2.00

THE NEW LOW-COUNTRY COOKING

THE NEW LOW-COUNTRY COOKING

125 Recipes for Coastal Southern Cooking with Innovative Style

COOKING

MARVIN WOODS

Foreword by Karen Hess

WILLIAM MORROW *An Imprint of* HarperCollins*Publishers*

HarperCollins books may be purchased for educational, business, or sales promotional use. For information please write: Special Markets Department, HarperCollins Publishers Inc., 10 East 53rd Street, New York, NY 10022.

FIRST EDITION

Designed by Leah Carlson-Stanisic

Foreword copyright © 2000 by Karen Hess
Photographs copyright © 2000 by Quentin Bacon

Printed on acid-free paper

Library of Congress Cataloging-in-Publication Data

Woods, Marvin
  The New Low-Country Cooking : 125 recipes for coastal southern cooking with innovative style / Marvin Woods; foreword by Karen Hess.—1st ed.
      p.   cm.
    Includes index.
    ISBN 0-688-17205-9
    1. Cookery, American—Southern style.   I. Title.
TX715.2.S68 W66 2000
641.5975—dc21

99–057545

00   01   02   03   04   QW   10   9   8   7   6   5   4   3   2   1

I would like to dedicate **The New Low-Country Cooking** to the following people who gave me inspiration, unconditional love, and support before, during, and after this book.

First and foremost to my Mom and Dad. Thank you for your love, encouragement, dedication, lots of hard work, and endless giving. You have shaped and molded me to strive, succeed, and be the best I can be. If not for you yesterday, I would not be who I am today. I love you and thank God for you both every day. To my oldest sister, Leslie, who is always there to do whatever she needs to do for her little bro—thanks for always being there. I love you. To my little sisters, who constantly give me inspiration, drive, hope, and sometimes a (loving) headache, Lyn, Erika, Tina, Cynthia, Monica, Lafern, and Lisa. Nothing can replace the bond and love we have for one another. Continue to keep it real. I love and thank you. To all my big brothers, who have lent an ear, a shoulder, and sometimes a backbone. Thank you for your strength, love, support, and the occasional subsidy, Kenny, Bayrob, Gregory, Mallory, Ricco, Dave, and Mark. To my loving partner in life and business, Petra. Thanks for your unconditional love, support, honesty, friendship, and the laughter. I respect, value, and love you all. Thank you for being in my life.

I would also like to dedicate **The New Low-Country Cooking** in loving memory to my great Aunt Tiny and Mom Wallace. You are forever in our memories.

Acknowledgments

Above all I give my praises to God Almighty, for without Him, none of this would be possible for me.

On a more earthly note I would like to thank the people who have had a significant amount of influence in my life, in the world of the kitchen.

There is an old African saying: "It takes a whole village to raise one child." In my case it was my immediate family and my extended family. Some of these people lived in my neighborhood and were blood relatives; some of these people didn't live near me at all but still had a major role in making me who I am today. They cared enough to make an effort. For that I would like to say thanks to you all. I'm only going to use your last names because if I don't, this list will be as large as the family cookouts we used to hold back in the Jersey days. Evanses, Perries (Howell and North Jersey), Fergusons, Hills, Hamptons, Collinses, Peaces, Stallworths, Homas, Owusus, and Olivers—your love, guidance, and concern has helped shape and mold me into what I am, and for that I say thanks and may God continue to bless you.

I would like to thank my culinary fraternity of brothers and sisters, who keep it real out in the restaurant field, for your support, encouragement, and in some cases, your teachings. You have been inspirational to me and have helped me in my mission to be a good chef: Marcus Samuelsson, Dirk Zephir, Monetta White, Norman Van Aken, Jonathan Eisemann, Michael Schwartz, Miles Shevitz, Mark Militelo, Bobby Flay, Douglas Rodriguez, Allen Susser, Frank Deletrain, Theodore Orsorio, Stephano Bastitini, Carolyn Flynn, Jean LaFont, Beth Valley, Jerri Banks, John Paul Demonico, Cary Neff, Timothy Dean, Rodney Renshaw, Ken Pittman, Herb Williams, Marvin James, Dave Lawrence, Fenol Marcelin, Lisa Cash, Derek Newton, Rochelle Brown, Cyndi Gammon, Frank Rourke, Frank Rowe, Scott Barton, Walter Hinds, Kimberly Brock Brown, and last but not least, the man who gave me my first break in New York, Peter Weiss.

My literary agent, Katharine Sands, believed in this project and in me from our first meeting. I deeply thank you for your dedication, guidance, encouragement, and for your commitment to bringing my book to fruition. I could not have become an author without you. And I thank Sarah Jane Freymann for additional support, generosity, and wise counsel.

Many writers signed on for the challenge of writing **The New Low-Country Cooking.** I thank you for your time, patience, input, and insight. The words aren't just words anymore—they are now this beautiful flowing cadence of technique, philosophy, history, and culture. Because of your dedication, hard work, professionalism, and passion, this project is truly southern exposure: Leah Sanders, Gail Lemke-Coyle, Barbara Albright, and my fourth-quarter all-star, Andria Scott Hurst.

Justin Schwartz believed in this project and shared my vision. Thank you, sir, for your talent, insight, support, hard work, and dedication to me and my project. Your efforts have been sincere, passionate, and invaluable. Elena Wiesenthal, Justin's assistant, I truly thank you for all of the passion, love, hard work, and dedication that you put into this project. It has been appreciated greatly, and I could not have made it without you. Thank you to the whole team at William Morrow for all your support and dedication. It has been a wonderful experience. This book would not be what it is without you guys. Thank you a thousand times. Special thanks to Harriet Bell, Karen Ferries, Carrie Weinberg, and Corinne Alhadeff.

I would also like to give special thanks to Beatrice, Julio, and the Il Bagatto staff.

Last but not least, I would like to thank my teacher, friend, author, and culinary historian Karen Hess, for it was you who started me on this informative highway leading to the great culinary heritage of the South and specifically the Low Country. Your words, teaching, seminars, and books are ever inspiring. I am so honored to know you, to have been able to work with you on this project, and to have you write my foreword. Thank you and may God continue to bless you.

May these few special paths that I have been fortunate to cross in life's journey continue to have God's blessings smile on them: Mona H., D-West, John Coyle, Ben A., Carl Van, Maria C., Cabria G., Kyle C., Bob, Robin and Nicole Greene, Saghi Z., Richard W., Alex Locadia, Karen and Jeff S., Roslyn S., Michael Vann and family, Angie Rae, Alexander Smalls, and Earl and Peter T.

As you go forth in life please remember, "The real tragedy is that we're all human beings, and human beings have a sense of dignity. Any domination by one human over another leads [to] a loss of some part of his dignity. Is one's dignity that big it can be crumbled away like that?"

—Yusuf Idris

Contents

Foreword
In Their Own Voices

At long last African-American cooks are being heard. In their own voices. Considering that going back to earliest Colonial times, black hands did the cooking in the South, it is high time. Their very presence in the kitchen of the Big House accounts for the near mythic qualities of Southern cookery as distinguished from the North. I have often discussed this factor, what the Chinese so aptly call wok signature, or wok presence, the almost mysterious differences in the final dish depending on who is "stirrin' the pots."

But in addition to that, those same black hands brought with them from Africa the skills of cultivating rice—not to mention cooking it, a finicky grain. They also brought with them their ways with okra or gumbo, cowpeas and their relatives (parading under myriad names such as field peas, black-bettys, red peas, black-eyed peas, and whippoorwills, but all from Africa), watermelon, benne or sesame seeds, sorghum, and so on. I have yet to mention that they also brought the use of a number of products that may have come here by way of the slave trade, such as eggplant (an old name being Guinea squash), and even New World products such as peanuts, perhaps even the tomato. Certainly they were chiefly responsible for the use of the American sweet potato, in large part because it resembled the yam of Africa insofar as its culinary properties were concerned. In short, the aromas of Africa came to characterize Southern cooking, and still do, this now close to 140 years after the departure of the African slave from the kitchen of the Big House.

It is not that their skills in the kitchen were unrecognized. Thomas Jefferson saw to it, for example, that James Hemings received professional chef's training in Paris; and a number of recipes attributed to him are found in the culinary manuscripts kept by Jefferson's granddaughters. Also there are occasional specific references to slave cooks, by name, in 19th-century cookbooks. But for the most part they were anonymous, their recipes appearing in works such as The Virginia

Housewife (1824) by Mary Randolph and The Carolina Housewife (1874) by Sarah Rutledge, without so much as by-your-leave. In Rev. Ebenezer W. Warren's introduction to Mrs. Hill's Southern Practical Cookery and Recipe Book, by Annabella P. Hill of Georgia, first published in 1867, we find something close to an acknowledgment: "A crisis is upon us which demands the development of the will and energy of Southern character. . . . As woman has been queen in the parlor, so, if need be, she will be queen in the kitchen." (Emphasis original.) He went on to say that "the race of good cooks among us is almost extinct," in an oblique reference to the end of slavery. He heralded the appearance of Mrs. Hill's cookbook as arguing "a new and brighter era in the culinary art."

What Rev. Warren was saying is that Southern women needed cookbooks. In the South it was emancipation that brought on the crisis; former slaves were choosing employment in factories rather than work under virtually feudal conditions as servants, leaving Madame to cope as best she could with unskilled immigrant labor.

In response there was an avalanche of cookbooks published in the last decades of the 19th century, and not only in the South; that is, the same thing was happening in the North, if not quite so precipitously. To be sure, there had long been published cookbooks, and a noble tradition it was in the South, but they had to be addressed to people who essentially already knew how to cook. Further, they were increasingly considered to be old-fashioned. This was a different era and housewives needed not only new instructions but far more detailed ones. The iron monster was replacing the hearth and the brick oven; milling techniques were changing, necessitating changes in baking procedures; food preservation techniques were changing; in short, everything was changing. Above all, they did not know how to cook.

Insofar as I can ascertain, What Mrs. Fisher Knows About Old Southern Cooking (1881) was the first of the post-bellum cookbooks to have been written by an African American, Abby Fisher, "Late of Mobile, Ala." By her own admission, she was illiterate, and her work had to be taken from dictation. The work is not only of major historical importance but a culinary treasure, far and away the best of the lot.

There have been other works by African Americans down through the decades, but aside from what I sometimes describe as the grand old ladies of American cookery, Edna Lewis of Virginia and Leah Chase of New Orleans, very few, until just the last four or five years, or so. We are now beginning to hear from a new generation of gifted black cooks, among them my friend Chef Marvin Woods, whose work I have the honor of introducing.

The women who had spent their lives cooking African-American dishes wrote about what they knew. They are true to their heritage, and it is beautiful. But those of this new wave of black chefs have new horizons, often feeling it is necessary to explain why they want to present a cuisine that is more structured, well, less African American, in a sense, or at least so it might be construed. I can understand their feeling of ambivalence, but they should not allow it to hobble their creativity. Marvin Woods is bringing his rich culinary heritage to the professional kitchen with flair, with élan, finally creating something authentically American in the sense that it arises from our own traditions, the best of our traditions insofar as culinary matters go. I believe James Hemings smiles on Marvin Woods and other African-American chefs who are engaged in establishing an identity, a visible presence, on the American restaurant scene. They have worked in the shadow of anonymity far too long. Let us hear more. In their own voices.

—Karen Hess
Culinary Historian

THE NEW **LOW-COUNTRY** COOKING

Introduction

Come with me on a delicious trip to one of the most fascinating regions in U.S. culinary history—the Low Country. It's the eighty-plus-square-mile area that extends inland from the coastal plain of South Carolina (Pawley's Island), southward to the Savannah River on the Georgia state line. If you've enjoyed Low-Country cuisine, you have eaten well. If you haven't, you're in for a treat. The coastal waters are rich with seafood such as bass, oysters, shrimp, clams, mullet, and sturgeon—caviar in their own backyard. The wooded marshy inlands make a great home for game birds such as pheasant, turkey, quail, and duck. The most important component of the magnificent food of the Low Country is rice.

Before I go on, let me tell you about myself and how I became familiar with this food. I am a descendent of Africa, the place where the roots of Southern and Low-Country cuisines run deep. But don't assume I grew up eating this food and knowing all about it. I am the son of Southern-born parents who live in the North. My career mom was not into cooking. It's in the last six years or so that I've come to know, appreciate, and respect the culinary contributions of my ancestors; and I am pleased to share them with you.

My own Southern exposure came when my family took summer road trips to the Carolinas. We'd enter my great-grandmother's house to the comforting scent of a wood-burning stove. More often than not there was a meal awaiting our arrival. I savored the aromas and flavors of yellow sweet corn, freshly baked breads, fried chicken, mustard greens, and juicy ripe watermelon.

I got my first taste of the kitchen in 1971—a time when scrambled eggs with ketchup was the delight of my culinary world. When my dad offered to let me help make them, I always jumped at the opportunity. He'd crack the eggs in a bowl and I'd whip them up. Then he'd pour the eggs in a frying pan and let me stand on a stool to stir them until they were done. I don't know what it was— maybe I was mesmerized by the blue gas flame—but it was enough to get me hooked. After that, I was in the kitchen whenever anyone was cooking.

It was around 1977 that Mom introduced me to the Betty Crocker recipe cards, and from that point my love and passion for cooking rose to another level. When one of my teachers realized I was taking my third year of home economics because I loved to cook (and not for easy credits), she suggested I apply to culinary schools. I was not sure about this at all.

Today that's a no-brainer, but you have to remember there was no 24-hour food network then. I don't know where Emeril was, but he wasn't on TV. Being a chef wasn't cool and hip at the time. I grew up in New Jersey, only 40 miles from one of the greatest cities in the world—New York. Our part of Jersey was rural and undeveloped. There were probably as many cows, chickens, and horses in the surrounding area as there were on a typical Southern farm. I didn't know about culinary schools, but I read the brochures.

After exploring my options, a trip to the Academy of Culinary Arts in Mays Landing, New Jersey, sealed the decision for me. The minute I walked into the school and looked into the classrooms, I knew this was the place for me. I saw ice carvings and advanced cake decorating. The aromas made me want to pull up a chair with knife and fork in hand to eat my fill and get an order to go.

One of the first lessons I learned about being in this business is its military-like structure. It's all about following a regimen, having self-control and discipline. I was anxious to cook right away. Sadly enough we didn't get to do that for about 3 months. We sat in a kitchen and took notes about food: how and where the food is produced, the right time to produce the food, and how to store the food. It wasn't what I expected, but looking back, it made perfect sense.

Finally we began learning about and making basic stocks and sauces. Those times in the kitchen were heavenly. Between classroom work and externships, graduation rolled around before I knew it. I was ready for the big time.

For the next few years I cooked in New York, England, and Ireland. I was working full-time, day and night. For a good part of my early career, I worked two jobs. It was like culinary grad school because I was learning so much at such a fast pace. My experience at Arizona 206, a restaurant serving upscale Southwestern cuisine, was a real eye-opener. I saw gourmet-style ingredients such as lobster, foie gras, and truffles paired with Southwestern herbs, spices, salsas, and cooking techniques.

That's when my thoughts stirred to do similar things using African and African-American influences and ingredients as the foundation. I started to experiment and get a sense of what I wanted my food to be. In 1995, as the executive chef of an elegant downtown Manhattan bistro, Cafe Beulah, I applied my cooking skills to my native food. I had the opportunity to explore and update **New Low-Country Cooking.** Now I am developing Diaspora Foods, the first product line to focus on the full scope of the African-American culinary heritage. I'm thrilled with the results. Now that you know me, let's explore the new Low-Country cuisine.

* * *

First, let's talk about rice. Rice played a vital role in the economic development of the Low Country and continues to be a daily menu item for most folks of the region. Rice has been cultivated in Africa since about 1500 B.C., as revealed in Daniel C. Littlefield's book Rice and Slaves. English settlers knew nothing about rice, but they knew of the skills of the West Africans. Slaves were brought to the Low Country by the tens of thousands, and with them came plants from their homeland. They could clear and prepare the rice fields, construct the canals and dikes, as well as manage the intricate flood-and-drain systems.

By the early 1700s the production of rice was hugely successful. Over 300 tons of the grain were shipped to England during the first years. The rice was quite beautiful in the fields, looking like a sea of molten gold. A rush of travelers, traders, and settlers moved to the Low Country to share the large profits of the rice called "Carolina Gold."

Southern cooking has always been multicultural. At its core are ingredients and cooking techniques from Africa, France, Spain, England, Germany, and the West Indies, as well as indigenous foods of the Native Americans. The African cooks of the Low Country achieved a level of sophistication in the blending of these cuisines that, years later, we realize helped to define American cuisine.

I feel that cooking is a dynamic art, with each generation making its own contribution. To make my food shine through, and to give it that extra lift, it must be close to my heart at all times. My European teachers would say to me, "Ah, it's just like mama used to make" and encourage me to "make it like your mama would make it." For me that meant that if you love what you do and do what you love, the results will be fantastic. No, this book is not an attempt to improve on the cooking of the old days; nothing could improve the perfection of my great-grandma's mustard greens and cornbread. Rather, it's a way to expand the appeal of Southern cuisine by incorporating international flavors and contemporary techniques.

My passion is reflected in the way I cook and present African-American food. My food. It's innovative and contemporary, with a touch of sophistication. I bring a fresh approach to old favorites as well as creating new ones. The dishes will seem at once different and familiar. I want to help you make and enjoy stellar food by practicing the following steps: Cook with love and passion; remember that simple foods can be simply delicious; and work on building flavor. The love and passion have to come from you—get excited about it, focus on the beauty of the ingredients. For simplicity, serve some foods unadorned to taste and see their natural beauty. The flavor-building thing may take a little time, but it will come with practice. Have fun with this, as you discover changes in your palate. Since our taste buds take on a new attitude about every seven years, you're probably ready for more complex flavors.

That's enough talk for now. Flip to a recipe that grabs you and let the burning begin. Let's Cook!

Stocks, Sauces, and Gravies

Southerners love to dress things up—their homes, themselves, and most decidedly their food. The less-is-more philosophy predominant in the foods of colder climates never had a chance in a region so rich in multicultural traditions and natural resources. Give a Southern cook a chance, and he or she will likely make a good dish better by adding a sauce, a gravy, or a carefully prepared stock.

Stocks are sometimes taken for granted, and that's not a good thing. Your end result can only be as good as your ingredients. Simply put, if you start with substandard ingredients to cut corners you'll be disappointed with the dish. When you make a little extra effort and start with a good stock, you'll turn out a marvelous sauce or gravy. One great thing about stock is that you can make it ahead of time and store it in airtight containers or self-seal bags in the freezer for months. Let these flavor enhancers get you started.

Chicken Stock

2 pounds chicken bones, rinsed
3½ quarts water
3 celery ribs, coarsely chopped
2 leeks, washed well and
  coarsely chopped

2 onions, coarsely chopped
2 carrots, coarsely chopped
2 bay leaves
1 clove garlic, cut in half
4 to 6 whole black peppercorns

Chicken stock can be used as a base liquid for soups, gravies, and sauces. It can be used in meat, fish, and vegetable recipes and of course with poultry. Some form of this basic ingredient is a must-have in the kitchen.

❋ ❋ ❋

In a large soup pot, combine all of the ingredients. Bring the mixture to a boil. Reduce the heat and simmer for 1½ hours, skimming the foam off the top as it rises. Strain the stock.

The stock is now ready to use. Or let cool, place in covered containers, and refrigerate for up to 1 week or freeze for up to 3 months. Skim off and discard any fat that has risen to the surface.

Veal or Beef Stock

6 pounds veal or beef bones
3 carrots, coarsely chopped
2 onions, coarsely chopped
1 celery rib, coarsely chopped
1 head garlic, cloves peeled and
 cut in half

1 cup tomato paste
1 bay leaf
6 whole black peppercorns
5 quarts water

Makes 2½ quarts

Making this stock from scratch will probably take a little more effort than any other stock—the reason being you will probably have to go to a butcher or a gourmet store to get the bones, and the cooking time is longer than for all other stocks.

* * *

Preheat the oven to 400°F.

Place the bones in a roasting pan. Roast the bones, turning them occasionally, until they start to brown, about 15 minutes. Stir in the remaining ingredients except the water and cook for another 20 minutes, or until the vegetables are brown.

Transfer the contents of the roasting pan to a large soup pot and add the water. Bring the mixture to a boil. Reduce the heat and simmer for 2½ hours, skimming the foam off the top as it rises.

Strain the stock and discard the bones and vegetables. Let cool, refrigerate, and then skim off and discard any fat that has risen to the surface. The stock is now ready to use. Or place in covered containers and refrigerate for 3 to 5 days or freeze for up to 3 months.

Vegetable Stock

Makes about 2½ quarts

Note: The vegetables listed as optional are good things to add, but not absolutely necessary to create a good vegetable stock.

2 tablespoons vegetable oil
4 celery ribs, cut into ½-inch pieces
2 carrots, cut into ½-inch pieces
1½ onions, cut into quarters
1 bunch parsley stems (optional)
1 rutabaga, cut into medium pieces (optional)
1 cup domestic mushroom stems (optional)
3 quarts water

Vegetable stock is one of those subtle ingredients I use for those times when I need a little liquid but don't want it to be too strong in flavor.

* * *

In a large soup pot, heat the oil over medium-high heat. Add the celery, carrots, and onions and cook until the vegetables begin to soften, 2 to 3 minutes. Add the remaining ingredients and bring the mixture to a boil. Reduce the heat and simmer for 40 minutes, skimming the foam off the top as it rises.

Strain the stock and discard the vegetables. The stock is now ready to use. Or let cool, place in covered containers, and refrigerate for up to 1 week or freeze for up to 3 months.

Fish Stock

3½ quarts water
5 pounds white fish bones
1 celery rib, coarsely chopped
2 leeks, washed well and
  coarsely chopped

3 onions, cut in half
1 bunch parsley
4 bay leaves
¼ cup whole black peppercorns

Makes about 2½ quarts

Fish stock can be used in sauces, stews, and soups that have seafood as the main ingredient.

* * *

Place all of the ingredients in a large soup pot and bring the mixture to a boil over high heat. Reduce the heat and simmer for 45 minutes, skimming the foam off the top as it rises.

Strain the stock and discard the solids. The stock is now ready to use. Or let cool, place in covered containers, and refrigerate for up to 7 days or freeze for up to 3 months.

Burner's Que

2 tablespoons vegetable oil
3 celery ribs, finely chopped
1 red bell pepper, seeded and finely chopped
1 green bell pepper, seeded and finely chopped
1 onion, finely chopped
4 cups coarsely chopped ripe tomatoes or tomato ketchup
1½ cups firmly packed dark brown sugar

½ cup prepared yellow mustard
¼ cup Worcestershire sauce
¼ cup fresh lemon juice
2 tablespoons garlic powder
2 tablespoons ground ginger
1 teaspoon chili powder
1 teaspoon cayenne pepper
1 teaspoon freshly ground black pepper
1 teaspoon salt

Barbecue sauce is a pivotal ingredient in Southern cooking. Just like marinara in Italian cooking or demi-glace in French, this sauce is an integral part of many Southern dishes. Originally, barbecuing was a technique for tenderizing tough cuts of meat. Large cuts of meat were seasoned and then placed over a low smoldering fire in a hole in the ground. The meat was cooked in this "pit" for 2 to 3 days, depending on the size of the piece of meat. As with many culinary concepts and techniques, barbecue has gone through an evolution or adaptation process. If you are jonzing for barbecue, you can usually get some form of it at your local fast-food or family-style restaurant, which may hold you over in a pinch, but *there is no substitute for real barbecue*. I'm not saying you have to dig a pit and watch your barbecue around the clock, but I do recommend that you season the meat, make your own sauce, and cook it over a low smoldering fire made of wood, coals, or a combination. Real barbecue is the epitome of Southern cooking and eating.

Brush this sauce over your meat or poultry, and offer it on the side as a tabletop staple. I like to brush it on a lush salmon fillet.

✳   ✳   ✳

In a large saucepan, heat the oil over medium heat. Add the celery, bell peppers, and onion and cook until the vegetables are slightly softened, 3 to 4 minutes. Add the tomatoes and brown sugar, reduce the heat, and simmer, stirring occasionally, until the sugar is completely dissolved. Add the remaining ingredients. Cover and cook over low heat for 1 hour, stirring occasionally. Check the seasoning, adding more salt if needed.

Let cool, store in an airtight container, and place in the refrigerator. It will last for months.

Creole Sauce

Makes 6½ cups

3 tablespoons vegetable oil
1½ cups fresh or frozen okra (approximately ¾ pound), finely chopped
1 cup finely chopped celery
1 white onion, finely chopped
1 red bell pepper, seeded and finely chopped
1 green bell pepper, seeded and finely chopped
1 cup fresh or frozen corn kernels
2½ quarts Vegetable Stock (page 8)
½ cup Brown Roux (page 15)
1 cup canned peeled whole plum tomatoes
2 tablespoons Marv's Hot Sauce (page 67) or your favorite store-bought brand

1½ tablespoons fresh thyme leaves, chopped, or 2½ teaspoons dried
1½ tablespoons fresh rosemary leaves, chopped, or 2½ teaspoons dried
1½ tablespoons fresh sage leaves, chopped, or 2½ teaspoons dried
1 teaspoon chili powder
1 teaspoon cayenne pepper
1 teaspoon Chili Paste (page 70) or Thai curry paste
1 tablespoon freshly ground black pepper
Salt and freshly ground pepper to taste

This is the base sauce I use for all of my gumbos (pages 25–28). It can be used for other stewlike dishes as well. It can also be used as a braising liquid or as a sauce to garnish salmon, snapper, chicken, and steak. This is a very versatile sauce!

Before we get into making this sauce, let me give a little background on the Creole style of cooking. The word "Creole" represents a group of people as well as a cooking style. In the early 1800s, when New Orleans was controlled by Spain, all residents of European origin were referred to as *Criollo*. Creole (*kree*-ohl) cooking was born at that time, simply from the combination of different ethnic groups living together in that region. African and Caribbean cooking is a common denominator in Creole cooking and some Southern (Low-Country) cooking—in both the ingredients used and the techniques. This style of cooking, influenced by French, Spanish, and African cuisines, generally relies on the heavy use of tomatoes, green peppers, onions, celery, cream, and butter.

* * *

In a large soup pot, heat the oil over medium-high heat. Add the okra, celery, onions, bell peppers, and corn and cook, stirring, until the vegetables start to soften, 5 to 7 minutes. Add the Vegetable Stock and bring the mixture to a slow boil.

When the liquid is boiling, remove about 1 cup and place it in a bowl. Add the Brown Roux to the 1 cup of stock and stir until it's combined and becomes paste-like. Gradually whisk this mixture back into the simmering liquid. Simmer for 15 minutes.

Add the tomatoes, hot sauce, herbs, chili powder, cayenne, Chili Paste, and black pepper. Taste and check the seasonings, adding salt and pepper if needed. Using a handheld blender, carefully blend all of the ingredients for 30 seconds. (This breaks up the okra and gives the mixture its classic gumbo consistency.) If you do not have a handheld blender, remove 2 cups of the ingredients and process in a blender or food processor. Be careful because the liquid is very hot. Return the puree to the soup pot.

Use the sauce immediately, or cool, cover, and refrigerate for up to 5 to 7 days. You can also freeze it in an airtight container; it will last for up to 2 months.

Three-Mustard Barbecue Sauce

Makes 4½ cups

2 tablespoons vegetable oil
3 celery ribs, finely diced
1 red bell pepper, seeded and finely diced
1 green bell pepper, seeded and finely diced
1 yellow bell pepper, seeded and finely diced
1 onion, finely diced
1 clove garlic, minced
2 cups firmly packed dark brown sugar

1 cup Dijon-style mustard
1 cup whole-grain mustard
1 cup prepared yellow mustard
Juice of ½ lemon
2 tablespoons Worcestershire sauce
1 tablespoon ground ginger
1 teaspoon chili powder
1 teaspoon cayenne pepper
Salt and freshly ground black pepper to taste

This is a good sauce to use on most meat dishes. It is especially good with chicken livers. Serve it at room temperature as a cocktail dipping sauce with shrimp or chicken wings.

* * *

In a large saucepan, heat the oil over medium-high heat. Add the celery, bell peppers, onion, and garlic, and cook, stirring, until they start to become soft, 3 to 5 minutes. Add the brown sugar and stir until it is dissolved. Stir in the three mustards and reduce the heat to low. Simmer for 10 minutes, stirring occasionally. Add the remaining ingredients except for the salt and pepper, and simmer 10 minutes longer, stirring frequently. Taste and check the seasoning, adding salt and pepper if needed.

Let cool, place in an airtight container, and refrigerate. It will keep for several months.

Brown Roux

1 cup (2 sticks) unsalted butter   1¼ cups all-purpose flour

Roux is used as a thickener in many different types of sauces, such as Creole and meat sauce. Brown roux has a rich nutty flavor that gives complexity and depth to whatever you are using it in. Making this roux requires cooking it a little longer than a regular roux. This takes away some of its strength, so when using this roux you will need to adjust your recipe accordingly.

* * *

Preheat the oven to 350°F.

Place the butter in a medium ovenproof saucepan and bake for 7 to 10 minutes, or until the butter is completely melted and starting to turn brown. Remove the saucepan from the oven and stir in the flour until it holds together. Place the saucepan back in the oven and bake until the mixture begins to turn brown, about 40 minutes. Let the mixture cool, and store in an airtight container in the refrigerator for up to 1 month.

As an alternative, you can prepare the roux on the stovetop: Place a pot on the stove over low heat. Add the butter and melt until golden brown. Stir in the flour and cook, stirring constantly, until the flour is light brown and has a nutty flavor, 5 to 7 minutes.

Demi-Glace Sauce

¼ cup vegetable oil
3 ribs celery, cut into small
pieces
2 medium onions (with skins),
cut into small pieces (about
1 inch long)
2 medium carrots with stems
removed, cut into small pieces
(about 1 inch long)

½ cup medium Madeira or
Sherry wine
¼ cup tomato paste
4¼ cups Veal or Beef Stock
(page 7)
3 tablespoons Brown Roux
(page 15)

Demi-glace is a wonderful adaptable sauce that can be used for a variety of meat and fish dishes. This sauce can be made up to a week in advance and it freezes well. Demi-glace works with many sauce innovations—try adding mushrooms, herbs, or lemon and see how your demi-glace can become many different sauces.

* * *

Pour the oil into a medium-size (8- to 9-inch) saucepan and heat over moderate heat. Add the celery, onions (with skins), and carrots and cook for 5 to 7 minutes. Stir occasionally until slightly brown. Add the wine. Add the tomato paste and stock. Simmer for 1½ hours, skimming the layer that forms on the top. Slowly stir in the brown roux and continue simmering over low heat for 15 to 20 minutes. Remove from the heat and strain.

Refrigerate for up to 7 days or freeze. Tip: freeze your demi-glace sauce in 3- or 4-ounce portions and use it to improvise meat and fish dishes.

Gingersnap Gravy

2 tablespoons vegetable oil
½ onion, finely diced
2 celery ribs, finely diced
1 tablespoon minced fresh ginger
¼ teaspoon freshly ground black pepper
1 quart Chicken, Veal or Beef Stock (depending on the meat you are serving, page 6 or 7)

4 to 6 Gingersnap Cookies (page 202), or use storebought cookies
Salt to taste

Makes 3 cups

This intriguing gravy is especially good with Chicken-Fried Steak (page 139) and other meat and poultry dishes.

* * *

In a medium saucepan, heat the oil over medium heat. Add the onion, celery, and ginger and cook, stirring, until the celery is softened, 5 to 7 minutes. Add the black pepper and heat through. Add the stock and bring the mixture to a boil. Reduce the heat and simmer for 15 minutes. Using a metal spoon, skim off any scum if it appears.

Break 4 cookies into crumbs in a heatproof bowl (preferably stainless steel). Take a ladleful of stock and gradually whisk it into the cookies. Mix in just enough liquid so that the mixture thickens slightly, and then gradually whisk back into the stock. Simmer for another 10 minutes. The mixture should be of gravy consistency. If it's not thick enough, repeat the cookie step using only 2 cookies at a time. Take care that the sauce does not get too thick too quickly. Taste and check the seasoning, adding salt if needed. Strain through a sieve. Let cool, and store in an airtight container. It will last up to 10 days in the refrigerator.

Pan Gravy

Meat juices left in pan
2 tablespoons corn, vegetable, or olive oil
2 medium onions, chopped
1 cup all-purpose flour

3 cups Chicken, Veal or Beef, or Vegetable Stock (pages 6, 7, or 8)
Salt and freshly ground black pepper to taste

Gravy is a sauce from meat juices, usually combined with a liquid such as chicken broth, beef broth, wine, or milk. It is then thickened with cornstarch or some other thickening agent. Pan gravy starts with the meat juices left in the pan after you have cooked the meat in it. A liquid is then added to the meat juice along with the thickening agent. Many gravies are strained, but not normally in the case of pan gravy.

* * *

Use the meat juices. In a large skillet, heat the oil over medium heat. Add the onions and cook, stirring, until they become translucent, about 5 minutes. Whisk in the flour and cook, stirring, until the flour starts to become light brown, about 3 minutes. Whisk in the stock and bring to a slow boil. Reduce the heat to low and simmer for 15 minutes, stirring occasionally. Taste and check the seasoning, adding salt and pepper if needed. Store in an airtight container in the refrigerator. This will last for up to 10 days.

 Soups

Southern soups truly are a melting pot of cultures. African, French, Spanish, Native American, and West Indian influences all show up in the bisques, chowders, and gumbos of Low-Country cooking. Okra is a requisite ingredient in any gumbo—be it meat, fowl, or seafood (gumbo is an African word for okra). Filé, ground sassafras leaves, was first used as a seasoning by the Choctaw Indians in Mississippi and came to be associated with Creole cooking and gumbo. Add the herb if you like, but it isn't necessary. As with preparing any good meal, the flavor lies in the freshness of the ingredients. (Hint: When making any seafood dish, avoid frozen fish and shellfish if at all possible.)

Pumpkin, Parsnip, and Butternut Squash Soup

Makes about 8 servings

2 tablespoons vegetable oil
1 onion, chopped
3 carrots, unpeeled, coarsely chopped
1 pound pumpkin, unpeeled, seeded and coarsely chopped
1 pound parsnips, unpeeled, coarsely chopped
½ pound butternut squash, unpeeled, seeded and coarsely chopped

7½ cups Chicken Stock or Vegetable Stock (page 6 or 8)
¼ cup chopped fresh sage leaves, or 2 tablespoons dried
¼ teaspoon ground nutmeg
½ teaspoon freshly ground black pepper
½ cup (1 stick) unsalted butter (optional)
Salt to taste

I love working with root vegetables because of their diversity. In this recipe, I blend the sweet and earthy flavors of three of my favorites to create a smooth warm-your-soul soup. This is the perfect soup to make in the fall or winter, when the ingredients are plentiful. Serve it in warmed soup bowls and garnish each bowl with a little sour cream and some croutons if you like. Marv Spice Croutons (recipe follows) add a nice touch of spiciness.

* * *

In a large soup pot, heat the oil over medium heat. Add the onion and cook, stirring, until it starts to soften, 5 to 7 minutes. Add the carrots and pumpkin and cook, stirring occasionally, until they start to soften, about 10 minutes. Add the parsnips and butternut squash and cook, stirring occasionally, until they start to brown, about 5 minutes longer. Add the stock. Increase the heat to medium-high and bring the mixture to a boil. Reduce the heat and simmer for 30 minutes, or until all the vegetables are soft. Add the sage, nutmeg, and pepper.

Remove the pot from the heat. Process the soup, in batches, in a blender or a food processor fitted with the metal chopping blade until smooth. Add the butter, if desired. Taste and check the seasoning, adding salt if needed. Strain through a medium sieve.

Butternut squash is best from early fall through the winter. When choosing these vegetables, select ones that are heavy for their size and have a hard, deep-colored rind free of blemishes or moldy spots. The hard skin of a winter squash protects the flesh and allows it to be stored longer than summer squash. It does not require refrigeration and can be kept in a cool, dark place for a month or more, depending on the variety.

Marv Spice Croutons

Makes 1 cup

4 to 5 slices day-old cornbread
  or white bread, crusts removed
2 teaspoons vegetable oil

1 teaspoon Marv Spice
  (page 64)

These croutons can take a soup or a salad a long way when it comes to adding flavor and texture.

＊　＊　＊

Preheat the oven to 375°F.

Cut the bread into ½-inch cubes and place in a bowl. Toss with the oil. Add the spice mixture and toss thoroughly. Place on a baking sheet and bake in the oven for about 4 minutes, or until golden brown. Let cool and serve, or store in an airtight container at room temperature for up to 3 days.

Asparagus Leek Soup

2 tablespoons vegetable oil
3 leeks, white parts only, well
   washed and coarsely chopped
1 onion, chopped
½ pound russet potatoes,
   unpeeled, coarsely chopped
2 pounds asparagus, trimmed
   and coarsely chopped

2 quarts Vegetable Stock
   (page 8)
¼ cup Roasted Garlic
   (page 73)
¼ cup (½ stick) unsalted butter
   (optional)
Salt and freshly ground black
   pepper to taste

Makes 6 to 8 servings

When I was growing up, asparagus wasn't one of my favorite vegetables. I do remember that one of the chefs in culinary school told me that the palate usually changes every 5 to 7 years. For me, the asparagus taste buds took a little longer to come around. Now I love asparagus—using it as a vegetable garnish, or in salads, or in this case as the main ingredient for a soup.

❋   ❋   ❋

In a large soup pot, heat the oil over medium heat. Add the leeks and cook, stirring, until they start to soften, about 5 minutes. Add the onion and cook, stirring, until it starts to soften, 2 to 3 minutes longer. Add the potatoes, asparagus, and stock. Bring the mixture to a boil. Reduce the heat to low and let simmer for 1 hour.

Remove the pot from the heat. Process the soup, in batches, in a blender or a food processor fitted with the metal chopping blade, adding the roasted garlic and butter, if desired, a little bit at a time. Check the seasoning, adding salt and pepper to taste.

Tomato and Fennel Soup

Makes 6 to 8 servings

Pernod is a liqueur that has a very distinct black licorice flavor. It is pale yellow in color and is often used in making French dishes or drinks.

2 tablespoons vegetable oil

½ pound (about 2 medium) fennel bulbs, chopped, fronds discarded

3 celery ribs, chopped

1 onion, chopped

2 cloves garlic, chopped

¼ cup Pernod liqueur (optional)

½ bunch fresh dill, stems removed (¼ cup trimmed)

I tablespoon celery seeds

½ teaspoon cracked black pepper

2 quarts Vegetable Stock (page 8)

3 pounds ripe tomatoes, or 3 cups canned peeled whole plum tomatoes, coarsely chopped

¼ cup (½ stick) unsalted butter (optional)

Salt to taste

I tend to use a lot of tomatoes, especially in the summer, when they are more flavorful. As children, we used to pluck tomatoes off the plants growing in our backyard. We'd give them a rinse with the garden hose, sprinkle them with a little salt, and eat them like apples.

* * *

In a large soup pot, heat the oil over medium heat. Add the fennel and cook, stirring, until it starts to soften, about 5 minutes. Add the celery, onion, and garlic. Cook, stirring, 5 minutes longer to allow the flavors to blend together. Carefully add the Pernod. (Caution! It could flame up.) Add the dill, celery seeds, and pepper. Add the Vegetable Stock and tomatoes, and bring the mixture to a boil. Reduce the heat to a simmer and let simmer for 40 minutes.

Remove the pot from the heat. Process the soup, in batches, in a blender or a food processor fitted with the metal chopping blade until smooth. Add the butter, if desired, and stir until melted. Taste and check the seasoning, adding salt if needed.

Vegetable Gumbo

2 tablespoons vegetable oil
2 cups thinly sliced fresh okra
2 celery ribs, diced
1 green bell pepper, seeded and chopped
1 red bell pepper, seeded and chopped
1 cup fresh or thawed frozen corn kernels
½ onion, chopped
3 cups Creole Sauce (page 12)

1 tablespoon finely chopped fresh thyme leaves
1 tablespoon finely chopped fresh rosemary leaves
½ cup chopped fresh or drained canned tomatoes
Salt and freshly ground black pepper, or Marv's Bay Spice (page 66), to taste
Hot cooked white rice

Creole Sauce is an important ingredient in this recipe. Prepare the sauce up to a week ahead of time and keep it refrigerated, or freeze portions, so you can easily put this soup together. Once you get this basic recipe down, you can experiment with any vegetables you like.

* * *

In a large soup pot, heat the oil over medium heat. Add the okra, celery, peppers, corn, and onions. Cook, stirring occasionally, until the vegetables start to soften, 5 to 10 minutes. Add the Creole Sauce. Bring the mixture to a boil. Reduce the heat and let simmer for 5 minutes. Add the herbs and tomatoes and simmer 5 to 10 minutes more. Taste and check the seasoning, adding salt and pepper or Marv's Bay Spice, if needed. Serve over rice.

Seafood Gumbo

3 tablespoons vegetable oil
2 celery ribs, diced
1 green bell pepper, seeded and chopped
1 red bell pepper, seeded and chopped
½ onion, chopped
1 cup corn kernels (preferably fresh)
2 cups thinly sliced fresh okra
1 pound striped bass or rockfish, cut into 1-inch pieces
½ pound mussels, scrubbed and debearded
1 pound jumbo shrimp, shelled and deveined
1 pound crabmeat (fresh, thawed frozen, or drained canned), well picked over

4 cups Creole Sauce (page 12)
½ cup chopped fresh or (drained) canned tomatoes
1 tablespoon finely chopped fresh thyme leaves, or ½ tablespoon dried
1 tablespoon finely chopped fresh sage leaves, or ½ tablespoon dried
1 tablespoon finely chopped fresh rosemary leaves, or ½ tablespoon dried
Salt and freshly ground black pepper to taste
Hot cooked white rice

With seafood gumbo, you can add anything from lobster to clams, from halibut to monkfish. (People, there is no limit—just technique.) Add lobster when you would the shrimp, though you will need to cook it a few minutes longer because it is thicker than shrimp. Be careful not to overcook your shellfish because it will turn rubbery on you. If you want to use clams, add them with the Creole Sauce and simmer until they open, just as you do with the mussels. You can use any type of white-flesh fish that has a similar texture to bass or rockfish—catfish, cod, sole, and snapper, to name a few.

＊　＊　＊

In a large saucepan, heat the oil over medium heat. Add the celery, peppers, and onion and cook, stirring, until everything starts to soften, about 5 minutes. Stir in the corn. Add the okra and cook, stirring, until it starts to soften, about 5 minutes. Add all the seafood and stir. When the shrimp begin to turn pink, after 2 to 3 minutes, add the Creole Sauce. Reduce the heat to a simmer. Add the tomatoes and herbs and cook until cooked through, about 5 minutes longer. Check the seasonings, and add salt and pepper to taste. Serve over hot rice.

Rockfish is often mentioned as a substitute for bass if bass is not available. It is a completely different fish, and there are many different varieties. If you are using rockfish, I recommend the types that are firmer in texture, such as yellowtail.

Mussels are in the mollusk family. They come in many varieties, which vary in shape, color, and size. The meat is usually a beige-white color and can be a little more rubbery than a clam or an oyster. I like to use mussels because I don't find them as "fishy" as clams or oysters.

Chicken and Sausage Gumbo

3 tablespoons vegetable oil
2 celery ribs, chopped
1 green bell pepper, seeded and chopped
1 red bell pepper, seeded and chopped
½ onion, chopped
1 cup corn kernels (preferably fresh)
2 cups sliced fresh okra
1 cup chopped boneless chicken (cut into ½-inch chunks)
7 ounces smoked sausage such as andouille, cut into ½-inch-thick slices

4 cups Creole Sauce (page 12)
½ cup chopped fresh or (drained) canned tomatoes
1 tablespoon fresh thyme leaves, or ½ tablespoon dried
1 tablespoon fresh sage leaves, chopped, or ½ tablespoon dried leaves
1 tablespoon fresh rosemary leaves, chopped, or ½ tablespoon dried leaves
Salt and freshly ground black pepper to taste
Hot cooked white rice

This combination of chicken and sausage is just one of the many that you can put together to make a good gumbo. If you want to substitute something for the chicken or sausage, by all means just use the recipe as a base and try something else. One suggestion: If you want to keep it on the health-conscious side, simply add more of the vegetables the recipe calls for or any other personal favorites.

* * *

In a large saucepan, heat the oil over medium heat. Add the celery, peppers, and onion and cook, stirring, until everything starts to soften, about 5 minutes. Stir in the corn. Add the okra and cook, stirring, until it starts to soften, about 5 minutes. Add the chicken and reduce the heat to a low simmer. Add the sausage, Creole Sauce, tomatoes, and herbs. Taste and check the seasoning, adding salt and pepper to taste. Simmer for 15 minutes, or until cooked through. Serve over hot rice.

Frogmore Stew

Makes 4 servings

For the stock

4 quarts water

2 cups shrimp shells (from 12 jumbo shrimp, see below)

2 onions, unpeeled, coarsely chopped

4 celery ribs, coarsely chopped

1 carrot, coarsely chopped

1 cup canned peeled whole plum tomatoes, undrained

3 tablespoons Marv's Bay Spice (page 66)

For the stew

2 tablespoons vegetable oil

1 green bell pepper, seeded and finely diced

1 red bell pepper, seeded and finely diced

2 tablespoons minced garlic

2 tablespoons minced shallots

12 jumbo shrimp, peeled (shells reserved for the stock) and deveined

1 pound duck sausage, cut into ½-inch pieces, or ½ pound spicy Italian sausage and ½ pound sweet Italian sausage, cut into ½-inch pieces

1½ cups chopped mustard greens

1½ cups chopped kale

1 tablespoon chopped fresh rosemary leaves, or ½ tablespoon dried

1 tablespoon chopped fresh thyme leaves, or ½ tablespoon dried

1 tablespoon chopped fresh sage leaves, or ½ tablespoon dried

4 ears fresh corn, cooked in boiling water for 15 minutes, then kernels removed from the cobs

1½ cups Cooked Lentils (page 103)

1 cup chopped canned peeled whole plum tomatoes

1¾ cups hot cooked white rice

There are no frogs in this stew. The name comes from the city of Frogmore, South Carolina. This dish is a bit labor-intensive, but once you get past that, you will thank me for turning you on to it.

continued

Combine all of the stock ingredients in a large soup pot. Bring the mixture to a boil over high heat and then reduce the heat to a simmer. Simmer for 30 minutes. Strain the stock and discard the solids.

In a large skillet, heat the oil over medium heat. Add the peppers, garlic, and shallots and cook, stirring occasionally, until the peppers are softened, 5 to 6 minutes. Add the shrimp and cook until pink, 1 to 2 minutes. Using a slotted spoon, remove the shrimp from the pan. Add the sausage, greens, and herbs and cook, stirring, until the greens start to wilt, about 3 minutes. Add the stock and corn and cook for 5 minutes. Add the lentils, tomatoes, and shrimp and cook for 30 seconds, just to heat through.

Divide the rice among 4 large bowls and ladle the stew over the top of the rice.

Cold Vegetable Soup

Makes 6 to 8 servings

2 pounds ripe beefsteak tomatoes, cored and coarsely chopped

2 cups V-8 juice

3 red bell peppers, seeded and coarsely chopped

2 cucumbers, seeded and coarsely chopped (or use seedless cucumbers)

2 celery ribs, coarsely chopped

1 green bell pepper, seeded and coarsely chopped

1 cup coarsely chopped Vidalia onion

1 carrot, coarsely chopped

¼ cup Worcestershire sauce

1 tablespoon Marv's Hot Sauce (page 67) or your favorite store-bought brand

1¼ teaspoons fresh lemon juice

1 teaspoon freshly ground black pepper

Salt to taste

Sour cream and cucumber slices, for garnish (optional)

This recipe is similar to the cold tomato soup called gazpacho. One of my great friends, Chef Ivan Dorvil, gave it to me and I tweaked it to make it work for me. It's delicious as an appetizer or salad course on a hot summer day.

* * *

Place all the ingredients except the salt and optional garnish in the container of a food processor fitted with the metal chopping blade. (Alternatively, you can use a blender and process the ingredients in batches.) Process until everything is blended together. Taste and check the seasoning, adding salt if needed. Serve in chilled bowls or mugs. Garnish each serving with a dollop of sour cream and a cucumber slice, if desired. Store leftovers in an airtight container in the refrigerator. This will keep for 3 to 5 days.

Navy Bean and Okra Summer Stew

Makes 6 to 8 servings

1 cup dried navy beans
2 bay leaves
2 cloves garlic
1½ quarts water
Salt to taste
1 teaspoon vegetable oil
2 thin slices bacon, finely chopped
1 onion, finely chopped
½ teaspoon minced garlic
1½ quarts Vegetable Stock (page 8) or water

2 teaspoons finely chopped fresh thyme leaves, or 1 teaspoon dried
1½ cups fresh or thawed frozen corn kernels
1 cup thickly sliced fresh or thawed frozen okra
3 medium tomatoes, seeded and coarsely chopped
Freshly ground black pepper to taste

I call this a stew because of its hearty consistency. Actually it is a fairly light dish. You can eat this by itself or serve it with rice and/or fish.

* * *

Rinse the navy beans well under running water, discarding any small stones or debris. Place the beans in a bowl and add enough water to cover by an inch or two. Let soak overnight.

Drain the beans. Place them in a medium saucepan and add the bay leaves, garlic cloves, and water. Bring the mixture to a boil, then reduce the heat to medium low and cook, partially covered, until tender but not mushy, about 1 hour. Season with salt about 10 minutes before the beans are done. Drain the beans, and discard the bay leaves and garlic.

In a large saucepan, heat the oil over medium heat. Add the bacon and cook until just crisp. Pour off any excess fat. Add the onion and minced garlic and cook, stirring often, until the onion is softened, about 2 minutes. Add the beans, vegetable stock, and thyme and simmer over medium-low heat for 15 to 20 minutes, or until the liquid is reduced by a third. Add the corn and okra and cook until tender. Stir in the tomatoes and cook until slightly softened, about 1 minute. Taste and check the seasoning, adding salt and pepper if needed.

Starters

Foods served before soup or salad are called "starters." Here they are the equivalent of appetizers, canapés, or hors d'oeuvres, but there is a difference. These starters can be altered to appear at different times during the meal. An ol' standby such as hushpuppies, for instance, can be stuffed with shrimp, oysters, or crab as a first course; served with cocktails before sitting down to dinner; or find their place at the table, to be enjoyed throughout the meal. Try doing that with a cucumber sandwich! My recipes for starters reflect the diversity of the Southern kitchen and lean toward the contemporary taste for light fare.

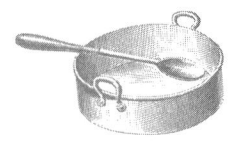

Shrimp Cocktail

Makes 6 to 8 servings

Often prawns are sold as large shrimp. The truth of the matter is that prawns are a different species. But not to worry, it is okay to use one as a substitute for the other.

6 quarts water
½ cup Marv's Bay Spice
   (page 66)
24 tiger prawns or jumbo
   shrimp, peeled and deveined

1½ cups Cocktail Sauce (recipe
   follows)

Shrimp are usually the seafood lover's favorite ingredient. There are two basic classifications for shrimp (this applies to most but not all species). Basically they are either warm-water or cold-water shrimp. The rule of thumb is, the colder the water, the smaller and tastier the shrimp. At the fish market, they are sold by the size (that is, how many to a pound); for example, 16/20's (which is the size I like to use) means you get 16 to 20 shrimp to a pound. I like this size because they tend to have good flavor and are large enough to have a good texture. Larger shrimp tend to have less flavor, and smaller shrimp generally turn into rubber balls if not cooked properly. In any case, if you have a favorite size of shrimp, use them; and if you use these and find that they aren't cutting it for you, know that there are enough species to keep experimenting with until you find one that does work for you.

* * *

In a large soup pot, combine the water and Marv's Bay Spice, and bring to a boil. Remove 2 quarts of the liquid; let it cool and then refrigerate. Bring the remaining 4 quarts of water back to a boil. When the liquid comes to a boil, add the shrimp and cook for 5 minutes, or until cooked. Using a slotted spoon, remove the shrimp and place them in the cooled liquid in the refrigerator for at least 12 to 15 minutes. When you are ready to serve them, use the slotted spoon to remove the chilled shrimp from the liquid. Serve with cocktail sauce.

Cocktail Sauce

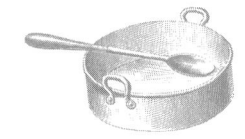

1 cup Burner's Que (page 10) or your favorite barbecue sauce
½ to 1 cup bottled horseradish, drained

1 tablespoon fresh lemon juice
Salt and freshly ground black pepper to taste

Makes about 1½ cups

This sauce is popular as a dip for seafood. It works well with clams, mussels, oysters, and lobster, and of course it's a winner with shrimp.

* * *

In a medium bowl, stir together all of the ingredients, adding salt and pepper to taste. Refrigerate for 1 hour. Serve in a bowl and let your guests dip in. Store in an airtight container. This will last for up to 2 weeks.

Doubled-Dipped Fried Okra

Makes 8 to 10 servings

If you've never seen okra before, it is green, about 3 inches long, and has ridged skin and a tapered cylindrical shape. In the South you can get this vegetable year-round, but the season for the rest of the country is from May through October.

1 pound fresh okra, washed
1 quart buttermilk
1 cup all-purpose flour
¾ cup stone-ground yellow cornmeal
½ teaspoon cayenne pepper
½ teaspoon chili powder
½ teaspoon freshly ground black pepper
1 teaspoon garlic powder
1 teaspoon salt
2 cups vegetable oil, for deep-frying

This recipe is my surefire weapon for turning people on to okra. Its crispy coating makes everyone a believer.

* * *

In a bowl or baking dish, combine the okra and buttermilk. In a shallow bowl or pie plate, stir together the flour, cornmeal, cayenne, chili powder, black pepper, garlic powder, and salt.

Using a slotted spoon or sieve, remove the okra, letting the excess buttermilk run back into the bowl. Place the okra in the flour mixture and toss to lightly coat. Remove the okra and, using a colander or sieve, shake to remove any excess flour. Return the okra to the buttermilk; repeat the procedure for a second coating.

Meanwhile, heat the oil in a 10- to 12-inch cast-iron skillet over medium-high heat until it registers 350°F on a deep-fat thermometer. (You can also test the heat by sprinkling a bit of flour into the hot oil to see if it bubbles.) When the oil is hot, add a large spoonful of okra to the skillet. (Don't use your hands because the coating tends to stick to your hands and will come off. And don't add too much okra at once or the oil will cool down and the okra won't cook properly.) Cook for 1½ minutes, then turn and cook 2 to 3 minutes longer, or until the okra is evenly browned on all sides. Using a slotted spoon, transfer the cooked okra to several layers of paper towels to drain. Repeat the procedure with the remaining okra. Serve immediately.

Black-Eyed Pea Cakes

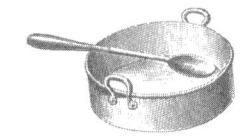

2½ cups cooked black-eyed peas
  (recipe follows)
2 tablespoons vegetable oil
½ onion, finely chopped
2 celery ribs, finely chopped
1 red bell pepper, seeded and
  finely chopped
1 green bell pepper, seeded and
  finely chopped
2¼ cups dry bread crumbs
  (preferably Japanese *panko*)

¼ cup sour cream
¼ cup mayonnaise
1 teaspoon chili powder
¼ teaspoon cayenne pepper
¼ teaspoon freshly ground black
  pepper
Salt to taste
3 large egg whites, lightly beaten
Vegetable oil for frying

Makes 12 to 14 cakes,
or 6 servings

Black-eyed peas are used all around the world in some type of fried cake form. Also known as cowpeas, they are boiled and pureed, then shaped into balls or cakes, deep-fried, and served on their own or as an accompaniment to a main course. Depending on the geographical location, there will be a different ingredient or two. The name also varies: These satisfying black-eyed pea cakes are called *akaras* in Nigeria, *akla* in Ghana, *ta'amia* in Ethiopia, and *gateaux-piments* in Mauritius. While black-eyed peas are really beans, they are called peas because they have more of a vegetable flavor than other beans. They are members of the mung bean family. Also known as black-eyed Susans, these beans have thinner skins than other beans and require less cooking. Try serving this favorite Southern specialty with Blackened Red Pepper Spread (page 77), hot sauce, sour cream, or a cream cheese–type spread.

* * *

Place 2 cups of the peas in the container of a food processor fitted with the metal chopping blade. Pulsing the motor on and off, process the peas just until they turn into a paste. (Don't puree the peas too much.) Place the pureed peas and the remaining whole peas in a large bowl.

Heat the 2 tablespoons oil in a medium saucepan over medium heat. Add the onion and cook, stirring occasionally, until slightly softened, 2 to 3 minutes. Add the celery and bell peppers and cook, stirring, until softened, 5 to 8 minutes. Add the cooked vegetables to the peas. Mix in ½ cup of the bread crumbs. Stir in the sour cream and mayonnaise until combined. Stir in the chili powder, cayenne, and black pepper. Taste, and add salt if needed.

Place the egg whites and the remaining 1¾ cups bread crumbs in separate shallow dishes. With a 2- to 3-ounce ice cream scoop or a large spoon, scoop up some of the mixture. Using your hands, roll the mixture into a firm ball, and then flatten the ball with the palm of your hand to form a miniature cake shape (about 2 inches in diameter and ½ inch thick). Roll the cake in the egg whites and then dip it in the bread crumbs. Repeat this process until you have used all of the pea mixture.

Preheat the oven to 350°F. Pour oil into a large heavy deep skillet to a depth of ½ inch. Heat the oil over medium-high heat until it registers 350°F on a deep-fat thermometer. (You can also test the heat by sprinkling a few bread crumbs into the hot oil to see if it bubbles.)

Cook the cakes for about 1 minute on each side, or until lightly browned. Using a slotted spatula, transfer the cakes to paper towels to blot off any excess oil. Place the cakes in a single layer on a baking sheet and bake for 7 to 10 minutes or until the centers of the cakes are hot.

Black-Eyed Peas

1½ cups black-eyed peas
2 celery ribs, cut in half
 lengthwise

½ onion, cut in half
1 carrot, cut in half
Salt to taste

Makes about 3 cups
cooked peas, or
6 to 8 servings

Black-eyed peas are a favorite in the South. They are beige in color and have a black circle at the top, resembling an eye. It is said that they first were brought here during the African slave trade. It has also been noted that they are originally from Asia. These peas can be purchased fresh or dried; the fresh ones will cook a little more quickly than the dried peas.

* * *

Place all the ingredients, except the salt, in a large saucepan and add water to reach about 1 inch above the peas. Cook over medium-low heat until the peas are tender (do not let them become too soft and mushy), about 1 hour. Remove the vegetables. Taste the peas and check the seasoning, adding salt if needed.

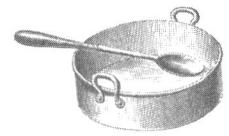

Hushpuppies

Makes 12 to 14 hushpuppies, or 6 servings

Variation

Shrimp or Oyster Hushpuppies: Prepare the batter, omitting the corn and adding a little more buttermilk to give a batter-like consistency. Dip shelled and deveined shrimp, or shucked oysters, into the batter and fry as directed.

Vegetable shortening or cooking oil for deep-frying
1½ cups yellow cornmeal
¼ cup all-purpose flour
¾ tablespoon baking powder
1 teaspoon baking soda
1 teaspoon ground coriander
½ teaspoon chili powder
½ teaspoon cayenne pepper
½ onion, grated
2½ cups buttermilk
3 large eggs, lightly beaten
¼ cup fresh or thawed frozen corn kernels

In the South, hushpuppies are typically eaten as a garnish. For instance, fried catfish and hushpuppies is a popular combination. I like to serve hushpuppies as an appetizer. These tasty mouthfuls are cornmeal dumplings that are deep-fried. Rumor has it that after the Civil War, when food was scarce, the cooks would fry up these dumplings and throw them out to the dogs to "hush them up." Once you put a basket of these bad boys on the table, you'll understand their quieting power.

*   *   *

Begin heating the shortening or oil in a deep-fryer or a cast-iron skillet over medium heat.

In a large bowl, stir together the cornmeal, flour, baking powder, baking soda, coriander, chili powder, and cayenne. Stir in the grated onion. Stir in the buttermilk, eggs, and corn until combined. The mixture will have the consistency of wet sand.

Heat the oil until it registers 375°F on a deep-fat thermometer. (You can also test the heat by sprinkling a bit of cornmeal into the hot oil to see if it bubbles.) Scoop up rounded tablespoons of dough and carefully drop them into the fat (in batches if necessary). Fry on one side until golden, 2 to 3 minutes. Turn and fry the other side until completely golden. Using a slotted spoon, transfer the cooked hushpuppies to several layers of paper towels to drain. Serve immediately.

Sautéed Chicken Livers

¾ cup all-purpose flour

1½ to 2 pounds chicken livers, cleaned

½ cup vegetable, corn, or olive oil

½ onion, finely chopped

1 teaspoon Marv Spice (page 64)

¼ cup bourbon

2 tablespoons chopped fresh parsley

1 tablespoon unsalted butter (optional)

Salt to taste

Makes 6 to 8 servings

My good friend Michael Vann (proprietor of Shark Bar and Soul Cafe in New York City) has an expression that applies perfectly to this dish: "It's cheap and deep." That means that the ingredients have been kept inexpensive, but the eater can feel them in his or her soul. Enjoy these livers by themselves or on top of some grits, mashed potatoes, or rice, with or without gravy.

❋ ❋ ❋

Place the flour in a shallow bowl or pie plate. Dredge the livers in the flour to lightly coat; shake off any excess.

In a medium skillet, heat the oil over medium-high heat. Add the livers and cook, stirring constantly, for 2 minutes. (Be careful—livers tend to make the oil pop and splatter.) Add the onions and cook, stirring constantly, for 1 minute more. Add the bourbon. Using a lit match, carefully light the bourbon and let it flame until the flame dies down. At this point, the livers will be medium-rare to medium. Cook longer if desired. Add the parsley, and the butter if desired. Toss everything together. Taste, and add salt if needed.

Duck Liver Spread

Makes 8 to 10 servings

3 tablespoons vegetable oil
1 pound duck livers
1 pound duck breast, skin removed, cut into 1-inch-thick slices
1 onion, finely chopped
1 tablespoon finely chopped fresh thyme, or ½ tablespoon dried

1 tablespoon finely chopped fresh sage leaves, or ½ tablespoon dried
1 tablespoon finely chopped fresh parsley
⅓ cup Madeira wine or bourbon
2 teaspoons Marv Spice (page 64)
Salt to taste

Here is my quick version of pâté. Usually pâtés are cooked in the oven for a couple of hours. In this recipe, even though the baking step is eliminated, it is still a slammin' dish.

* * *

In a large skillet, heat the oil over medium-high heat. Add the duck livers, taking care that the oil doesn't splatter, and cook, stirring constantly, until they are completely cooked, 7 to 10 minutes. Using a slotted spoon, remove the livers from the skillet and reserve. Add the duck breast slices and cook until they are medium cooked, 5 to 7 minutes. Using a slotted spoon, remove the duck from the skillet.

Add the onions, herbs, and wine to the skillet. Using a lit match, carefully light the wine and let it flame until the flame dies down. Return the duck livers to the skillet and add the Marv's Spice. Cook for 3 minutes longer to allow the flavors to blend. Remove from the heat and let cool a bit.

In the container of a food processor fitted with the metal chopping blade, or in a blender, process the liver mixture with the duck breast slices until smooth. Check the seasoning, and add salt if needed. Serve at room temperature on toast or use as a dip. Store in an airtight container in the refrigerator for up to 7 days.

Pickled Shrimp

2 pounds medium shrimp,
  shelled and deveined
3 Vidalia onions, thinly sliced
¾ cup white balsamic vinegar
  or champagne vinegar
½ cup vegetable oil
Juice of 2 lemons
2 tablespoons salt

2 tablespoons granulated sugar
1 tablespoon Dijon-style mustard
1 tablespoon crushed red pepper
  flakes
1 tablespoon celery seeds
1 tablespoon freshly ground
  black pepper

Makes 6 to 8 servings

Using vinegar, spices, and brine to pickle foods for later use is a technique that is as common in the South as it is in Africa, the Caribbean, Spain, and Portugal. Combined together, the vinegar, salt, and citrus act like a cooking agent. This is very similar to the Spanish version, called seviche. If you do not feel comfortable using raw shrimp, or would like to speed up the recipe, use precooked shrimp instead and cut the marinating time to 4 hours.

* * *

In a large noncorrosible dish, arrange the shrimp in a single layer. Cover the shrimp with the sliced onions.

In a medium bowl, mix together all the remaining ingredients. Pour the mixture over the shrimp, making sure that they are completely submerged. Cover and refrigerate for at least 24 hours (at least 4 hours if using cooked shrimp) but no more than 36 hours. Serve with cocktail sauce or wedges of fresh lemon. Store the shrimp in an airtight container in the refrigerator for up to 3 days.

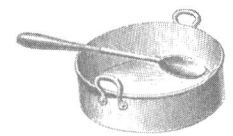

Fried Vidalia Onion Rings

Makes 6 to 8 servings

For the buttermilk marinade
1¼ quarts buttermilk
2 tablespoons Marv Spice
   (page 64)
1½ tablespoons onion powder
1½ tablespoons garlic powder
3 Vidalia onions, cut into
   ¼-inch-thick slices and
   separated into rings

For the bread crumb mixture
2 cups all-purpose flour
1 cup dried Japanese *panko* bread
   crumbs
2 tablespoons salt

For frying
2 cups vegetable oil

These particular onions get their name from Vidalia, Georgia. They are at their peak during May and June. I love working with Vidalias because they are a lot sweeter and juicier than most onions. I double-dip these onion rings to make them extra-crispy.

* * *

In a large bowl, stir together the buttermilk, Marv Spice, onion powder, and garlic powder. Place the onion rings in the bowl and submerge to coat completely.

In a shallow bowl or pie plate, combine the flour, bread crumbs, and salt.

Using a slotted spoon, remove the onion rings from the marinade, letting the excess liquid run back into the bowl. Add 5 to 6 onion rings at a time to the bread crumb mixture and lightly coat both sides; shake off any excess. Return the onion rings to the buttermilk and repeat the procedure for a second coating.

Meanwhile, in a 10- to 12-inch cast-iron skillet, heat the oil over medium-high heat until it registers 350°F on a deep-fat thermometer. (You can also test the heat by sprinkling a bit of cornmeal into the hot oil to see if it bubbles.) Using a large spoon, carefully add 5 to 6 onion rings to the skillet. (Don't use your hands because the coating tends to stick to your hands and it will come off. And don't overcrowd the onion rings in the pan, or they won't cook properly.) Cook for about 1½ minutes, then turn and cook about 1½ minutes longer, or until the onion rings are evenly browned on both sides. Using a slotted spoon, transfer the cooked onion rings to several layers of paper towels to drain. Repeat the procedure with the remaining onion rings.

You can dip these in sour cream or any dip that you use for chips.

Vidalia onions grow in and get their name from Vidalia, Georgia. They are pale yellow and are very sweet. You can also use other sweet onions in season like Walla Walla or Maui. If they are not available at your local supermarket, you can mail-order.

Salads

Historically, in Southern cooking salads were used as a "refresher course" to cleanse and reinvigorate the palate before embarking on the main course. Taking its cue from French cuisine, a salad was best served pure and simple: a good local lettuce like pepper grass, chervil, or cress and a fresh vinaigrette dressing. But the varied vegetables—and, yes, fruits and nuts—of Southern environs, particularly the Low Country, made the salads extraordinary. European and Asian settlers brought with them then-exotic vegetables like tomatoes and asparagus, which when complemented by the region's native greens, produced salads of unparalleled complexity in the colonies. Interestingly, while it seems the merits of olive oil have only recently been discovered by most Americans, the Low Country has always sung its praises as a salad's dressing and as an ingredient in cooked dishes. In fact, olive trees grow wild in this region (a legacy of early Spanish settlers), though the soil is usually too rich to allow the trees to produce. Thus, olive oil was traditionally supplied by Mediterraneans, visitors and settlers both. You'll find that lemon juice or sherry vinegar is the perfect complement to an olive oil–based Southern-style salad dressing.

Shrimp Salad with Lemon Oil Dressing

Makes 6 to 8 servings

4 cups mixed salad greens, such as mesclun
2 tablespoons finely chopped fresh parsley (preferably flat-leaf)
3 tablespoons fresh lemon juice
1½ tablespoons olive oil
1½ tablespoons sparkling water, seltzer, or club soda
½ teaspoon freshly ground black pepper
Salt to taste
16 jumbo shrimp (16 to 20 per pound), peeled, deveined, and poached (recipe follows)

This salad is a perfect example of what I was referring to in the introduction to this chapter: It's light and refreshing. You can serve this as a starter, or you can serve it after the main course—either way you will come up a winner. I always combine the stronger-flavored greens like arugula or frisée with something that is milder or neutral like Romaine, oak, butter, or even iceberg lettuce.

* * *

Place the salad greens and parsley in a large bowl. Drizzle the lemon juice, olive oil, and sparkling water onto the leaves and toss. Add the pepper, and salt to taste. Arrange the salad on serving plates.

Toss the shrimp in the dressing that remains in the salad bowl, and distribute them over and around the salad. Using a spoon, drizzle any remaining dressing over the shrimp.

Poached Shrimp

6 quarts water
¼ cup Marv's Bay Spice
  (page 66)

2 tablespoons salt
24 tiger prawns or jumbo
  shrimp, peeled and deveined

Makes 6 to 8 servings

This is a quick and easy way to prepare shrimp. You can eat these hot as they are, or you can chill them and eat them with a dipping sauce, or in this case with a salad. You can also use this method as a short cut to making other dishes that call for shrimp.

* * *

In a large soup pot, combine the water, Marv's Bay Spice, and salt and bring to a boil. Transfer 2 quarts of the water to another container, and cool in the refrigerator.

Bring the remaining 4 quarts of liquid back to a boil. When the liquid comes to a boil, add the shrimp and cook for 5 minutes or until cooked. Using a slotted spoon, remove the shrimp and place in the cooled liquid in the refrigerator for at least 15 minutes.

When you are ready to serve the shrimp, use the slotted spoon to remove them from the liquid.

Wilted Greens with Herb Vinaigrette

Makes 6 servings

Kale comes frozen, canned, and fresh. The leaves also come in all sorts of colors—usually deep green with shades of blue and purple running through them. This is another winter vegetable that you will be able to find in certain markets year-round. Kale may be prepared in any of the ways you might cook spinach. When using fresh kale, be sure to remove the center stem.

2 tablespoons vegetable oil
1 tablespoon minced onion
½ cup finely chopped cooked smoked bacon (optional)
4 pounds fresh spinach leaves, coarsely chopped if large
4 pounds fresh kale leaves, coarsely chopped

⅔ cup sparkling water, seltzer, or club soda
Salt and freshly ground black pepper to taste
¾ cup Herb Vinaigrette (recipe follows)

This is a good, versatile salad, meaning you can serve it just as a salad or you can serve it alongside meat, fish, or poultry. You can also add meat, fish, or poultry to the salad to make it a full meal.

When I make a wilted salad I toss the greens quickly in the pan and then remove them because I like the different textures of some wilted and some not so wilted. I suggest that you use a large pan, and when you add the first batch of greens to the pan, be sure to stir them or the ones on the bottom will cook more than the ones on the top. Bacon is optional for those of you who are watching your diet, but I will say that bacon is the one ingredient that makes this a true Southern salad.

* * *

In a large sauté pan, heat the oil over medium heat. Add the onion and cook, stirring, until softened, about 2 minutes. Add the bacon and stir for about 1 minute. Stir in the greens and sparkling water, and cook for 1 to 2 minutes, depending on how fully wilted you would like the greens. Remove from the heat and transfer to serving plates or bowls. Add salt and pepper to taste, drizzle 2 tablespoons of the dressing over each salad, and serve.

Herb Vinaigrette

¼ cup white wine vinegar
2 tablespoons finely chopped
  fresh parsley
2 tablespoons finely chopped
  fresh cilantro
2 tablespoons finely chopped
  fresh thyme

1 tablespoon minced garlic
1 teaspoon salt
1 tablespoon freshly ground
  black pepper
1 cup corn, vegetable, or
  olive oil

Makes 1 cup

Thyme has gray-green leaves that give off a pungent minty, light-lemony aroma. You should be able to get this year-round at your local supermarket.

This dressing is easy to make and very good on anything from fish to salad greens.

＊　＊　＊

Place all of the ingredients except the oil in a medium-size bowl.
  Slowly whisk in the oil, using a wire whip. Taste and adjust the seasonings if necessary. Place in an airtight container and store in the refrigerator for 2 to 3 weeks.

Cole Slaw

½ small head green cabbage, shredded
½ small head red cabbage, shredded
½ head Napa cabbage, outer leaves only, shredded (or use more green cabbage)

½ to 2 carrots, shredded
¾ cup Marv's Slaw Dressing (recipe follows)

I'm sure many of you would like to believe this is a true Southern dish. Well, believe it or not it comes from the Dutch. The word *koolsla* means "cool cabbage." This salad has many different versions, but as long as the base is shredded red or white cabbage, you can put anything from pickles to bacon in it and call it cole slaw.

* * *

Combine all the vegetables, except a half handful of shredded carrots, in a large bowl.

Pour in the dressing and toss. Transfer the cole slaw to serving dishes. Garnish the top of each salad with the remaining shredded carrots.

Marv's Slaw Dressing

½ cup heavy cream
¼ cup mascarpone or cream
  cheese, at room temperature
2 tablespoons honey
1 teaspoon salt
¼ teaspoon celery seeds

1 tablespoon white balsamic
  vinegar or sherry vinegar
½ tablespoon Dijon mustard
½ teaspoon freshly ground black
  pepper

Makes 1 cup

* * *

Place the heavy cream in a medium bowl. Stir in the mascarpone, using a wire whisk, until smooth. Add the rest of the ingredients and mix thoroughly.

Store in an airtight container, refrigerated, for up to 2 weeks.

Cucumber Shoestring Salad

Makes 6 to 8 servings

Cucumbers may be found year-round, with their peak being May to August. You can eat them with their skin on or off. When choosing cucumbers, look for firm, smooth, deep green skin. Avoid those that have soft spots. The smaller the better, because as cucumbers age, their seeds become large and bitter.

Note: Cut the cucumbers across, forming 2-inch logs. Slice each log lengthwise into ¼-inch-thick slices. Lay the slices flat and cut them into thin strips, discarding the seeds. You can also use a mandoline: cut the logs lengthwise on the julienne blade until you reach the seeds.

2 cucumbers, peeled and julienned (see Note)
½ pound Japanese soba (buckwheat) noodles, cooked according to package directions
½ cup canned unsweetened coconut milk
Juice of 1 lime
2 tablespoons oyster sauce
2 tablespoons soy sauce
2 tablespoons tahini (sesame paste)

2 tablespoons light sesame seeds
1 tablespoon Asian-style sesame seed oil
1 tablespoon chopped fresh cilantro
2 teaspoons honey
1 teaspoon minced fresh ginger
½ clove garlic, minced
¼ teaspoon crushed red pepper flakes
Salt and freshly ground black pepper to taste

In the early and mid 1700s, Chinese immigrants settled in Charleston and in the Low Country. They came as traders of spices and brought with them soy and ginger, flavors which were then incorporated into the melting pot of Low-Country cuisine.

* * *

In a large bowl, combine the cucumber strips with all the remaining ingredients. Taste and check the seasoning, adding salt and pepper if needed.

Macaroni Salad

1½ pounds elbow macaroni, cooked according to package directions, drained, and cooled

½ cup sweet pickle relish

½ cup finely chopped celery

¼ cup finely chopped onion

¼ cup finely chopped red bell pepper

¼ cup finely chopped green bell pepper

¼ cup mayonnaise

2 tablespoons Dijon-style mustard

1 teaspoon Worcestershire sauce

1 teaspoon fresh lemon juice

1 teaspoon Marv Spice (page 64)

½ teaspoon celery salt

Salt and freshly ground black pepper to taste

Most macaronis are tube-shaped, but there are other forms including shells, twists, and ribbons. Elbows are, of course, the favorite. Beware—most macaronis double in size during cooking.

This is one of the celebrated salads of the South. Whether it is an indoor or an outdoor function, you will usually see a few different versions of this salad. I also like to add flaked crabmeat or fresh tuna to this basic recipe. Other ingredients to think about using are ham, boiled eggs, sausage, and tomatoes.

❋ ❋ ❋

Place the macaroni in a large bowl. Add the remaining ingredients and stir gently to combine. Taste and check the seasoning, adding salt and pepper if needed. Because of the mayonnaise, I serve this salad chilled. It can be stored in an airtight container in the refrigerator for 7 to 10 days.

Asparagus and Summer Tomato Salad

Makes 8 servings

2 pounds asparagus
¾ cup water
½ teaspoon salt
2 pounds large ripe tomatoes, chopped
½ onion, finely chopped
¼ cup garlic-infused oil

2 tablespoons balsamic vinegar
¼ cup chopped fresh parsley
1 teaspoon freshly ground black pepper
½ teaspoon Dijon-style mustard
Salt to taste

If you want to enjoy this salad when it is at its best, make it when garden-fresh tomatoes are at their peak. It can be served alongside an entrée, or you can serve it as a salad. If serving it as a salad, I recommend drizzling a little White Balsamic Vinaigrette (page 59) over the top.

* * *

Bend each stalk of asparagus to snap off the tough base portion. If the asparagus are especially tough, peel the stalks with a vegetable peeler. Wash the asparagus in water, rinsing well so that no grit remains.

In a large skillet, bring the water and salt to a boil. Add the asparagus, cover, and simmer until the stalks are crisp-tender, 6 to 8 minutes. Drain.

In a large bowl, stir together the tomatoes and onion. In another bowl, stir together the garlic oil, vinegar, parsley, pepper, and mustard. Add this mixture to the tomatoes. Taste and check the seasoning, adding salt if needed.

Arrange a few stalks of cooked asparagus on each salad plate. Top with a spoonful of the tomato mixture and serve.

White Balsamic Vinaigrette

2 tablespoons pureed Roasted
  Shallots (page 74)
2 tablespoons Dijon mustard
1 tablespoon finely chopped
  Roasted Garlic (page 73)
½ cup white balsamic vinegar
  (or use red balsamic)

1 cup vegetable oil
1 tablespoon sparkling water
Salt and freshly ground black
  pepper to taste

Makes about 1 cup

I use sparkling water because the carbonation in the water aerates the dressing. This gives it a lighter texture and taste.

This dressing works well with vegetables, leafy-type salads, and poultry, meat, and fish dishes. You should be able to find white balsamic vinegar at your local grocery. This dressing would work nicely with the Shrimp Salad (page 50).

* * *

Place the shallots, mustard, and garlic in a medium bowl. Add half of the vinegar. Add the oil in a steady stream, whisking continually, until the dressing starts to thicken. Then add the remaining vinegar and whisk in the rest of the oil. Add the sparkling water. Taste and check the seasoning, adding salt and pepper if needed. Store in an airtight container in the refrigerator for 2 to 3 weeks.

Baby Red Romaine, Arugula, and Couscous Salad with Balsamic Syrup

Makes 6 to 8 servings

For the balsamic syrup
1 tablespoon vegetable oil
1 small onion, chopped
1½ cups balsamic vinegar
¼ cup honey

For the salad
8 ounces baby red Romaine
8 ounces arugula

1½ cups couscous, cooked to
    yield 2 cups (page 95)
Salt and freshly ground black
    pepper to taste
1 cup teardrop, currant, or
    cherry tomatoes, cut in half

In this salad, the two different salad greens balance each other out. The reason why you start with so much vinegar is because you will be reducing it on the stove for approximately 40 minutes. The syrup has an intense flavor. It is great for salads, but drizzle a little bit over a piece of fish and see the reaction!

*　*　*

In a small saucepan, heat the oil over medium heat. Add the onion and cook, stirring, until translucent, 2 to 3 minutes. Add the balsamic vinegar and the honey. Reduce the heat to low and simmer until the liquid becomes syrupy, about 40 minutes. It should reduce to two-thirds of the original amount. Remove the pan from the heat and cool to room temperature.

Wash the salad leaves in cold water and dry thoroughly. Place the leaves in a medium bowl. Add the couscous and the balsamic syrup and toss gently to combine. Add salt and pepper if needed. Arrange the salad on plates, add the tomatoes, and serve.

The syrup can be stored in an airtight container at room temperature for up to 14 days. (You don't want it to be completely chilled or you will have to reheat it.)

Potato Salad

3 pounds red bliss potatoes, cut into ½-inch cubes
3 hard-boiled eggs, chopped
2 celery ribs, finely chopped
½ cup sweet pickle relish
½ cup mayonnaise
2 tablespoons Dijon-style mustard
1 teaspoon paprika
½ teaspoon celery salt
Salt and freshly ground black pepper to taste

Makes 10 to 12 servings

Potato salad is one of the most-requested dishes for potluck dinners and other large gatherings. A couple of professional tips for you when making your potato salad: Try using new potatoes, because they tend to hold their shape better than most other potatoes. After you boil the potatoes, let them cool all the way down; the potatoes will absorb too much dressing if they are hot.

* * *

Cook the potatoes in a large pot of boiling salted water just until tender, 20 to 30 minutes. Drain and set aside to cool completely. Place the cooled potatoes in a large bowl. Add the remaining ingredients and stir gently to combine. Taste and check the seasoning, adding salt and pepper if needed. Serve chilled. Store in an airtight container in the refrigerator for up to 10 days.

Fresh Fruit Summer Salad

3 fresh Georgia peaches,
  unpeeled, sliced
3 bananas, peeled and sliced
½ pint strawberries, hulled
1½ cups cubed fresh pineapple
  (or canned if you like)
½ pint blueberries

¼ cup Simple Syrup (page 210)
1 teaspoon fresh lemon juice
2 tablespoons finely chopped
  fresh mint
¼ teaspoon freshly ground black
  pepper

This can be served as an opener, or it can be served as a closer, meaning as a dessert. If you are serving the salad as a dessert, simply sprinkle a little confectioners' powdered sugar over the top before you serve it. This salad is great in the summer, when the fruit is at its best.

* * *

Combine all the ingredients in a large bowl, and use your hands to lightly toss them together. Place in the refrigerator for 15 to 20 minutes to chill. Serve in small bowls.

Condiments

The cities of Savannah and Charleston have long enjoyed exotic foods that the rest of the country is just now catching on to. The African cooks who once ruled the kitchens liberally borrowed flavors from the best of English, Greek, French, and Mediterranean cuisines to add to their own. Nowhere does this fusion reveal itself more than in their condiments. Lovely complicated chutneys were learned from traders plying the Indian Ocean. Okra, native to Africa, was pickled as a crunchy snack or combined with other ingredients to make a relish.

These recipes for chutneys, spice mixtures, and relishes are perfect for dressing up a supper's main course, or for adding a bit of panache to a breakfast or lunch. Properly refrigerated, these condiments will last for weeks.

Marv Spice (Savory)

Makes ¼ cup

Note: You really don't want to use the mixture past that 6-month time period because the spice will lose its intensity.

1 tablespoon ground nutmeg
1 tablespoon chili powder
1 tablespoon cayenne pepper

1 tablespoon celery salt
¼ teaspoon freshly ground black pepper

I use this spice mixture in my Macaroni and Cheese (page 94) as well as in fish, chicken, and meat dishes that I feel can use a touch of inspiration.

* * *

In a small bowl, mix all of the ingredients together until combined. Store in an airtight container for up to 6 months.

Marv's Sweet Spice

1 teaspoon ground nutmeg
1 teaspoon ground cinnamon
1 teaspoon vanilla powder
(available in specialty food
stores)

2 tablespoons firmly packed light
brown sugar

Makes 3 tablespoons

Note: I wouldn't use this
mixture after 3 months
because the vanilla
powder will lose its
intensity.

Here's a versatile spice that is perfect for sprinkling on a variety of baked fruit desserts such as cobblers, pies, and fruit tarts. Sprinkle it over the surface of the pastry before baking.

* * *

In a small bowl, mix together all the ingredients until combined. Store in an airtight container for up to 3 months.

Marv's Bay Spice

Makes about 1½ cups

Note: Make sure that the coffee mill you use is dedicated to grinding only seeds, spices, and dried herbs.

¼ cup yellow mustard seeds
8 medium bay leaves
2 tablespoons black peppercorns
2 tablespoons crushed red
    pepper flakes
4 teaspoons celery seeds

1 tablespoon coriander seeds
1 tablespoon ground ginger
1 teaspoon ground mace
¼ cup salt
2 tablespoons chili powder
2 tablespoons cayenne pepper

Old Bay is a prepared seasoning mixture that is available at supermarkets. Here is my homemade version. It's great for dressing up soups and stews, and especially fish. One of the main ingredients in this seasoning is bay leaves. In addition to using bay leaves for flavoring foods, Africans also believe bay leaves aid digestion.

* * *

Using a spice mill, a mortar and pestle, or a coffee mill (see Note), process the mustard seeds, bay leaves, peppercorns, red pepper flakes, celery seeds, and coriander seeds until ground to a powder. Pour the mixture into a medium bowl and stir in the remaining ingredients. Store in an airtight container. The mixture is good until you use it up, as long as it is kept dry and sealed.

Marv's Hot Sauce

10 carrots, juiced (about 3 cups juice), or 3 cups store-bought carrot juice
¼ cup Dijon-style mustard
¼ cup honey
3 tablespoons balsamic vinegar

2 tablespoons Chili Paste (page 70), or more to taste, or 3 to 4 tablespoons Tabasco Sauce
1½ teaspoons freshly ground black pepper
Salt to taste

Makes about ¾ cup

Note: Be aware that we are dealing with fresh carrot juice as the main ingredient for this recipe; it may sour after the 7-day storage period.

Hot sauce was and still is a favorite condiment throughout Africa and most of the Southern states. Africans use a lot of different types of peppers to spice up their foods when they cook. They believe that hot sauce has health-giving qualities, such as reducing high blood pressure.

Here in the States, chile peppers are grown in abundance in the Georgia region, and a lot of the commercial hot sauces on the market today are produced in the South. In Southern homes, hot sauce is frequently used on greens, fried chicken, pork chops, fried shrimp, and shrimp cocktail. It has unlimited uses as a seasoning. It's healthy and it's hot.

*　*　*

Mix all the ingredients together in a noncorrosible bowl. Check for seasoning and add salt if needed. The sauce is ready for use. Store in an airtight glass container and refrigerate for up to 7 days.

Pickled Okra

Makes 5 cups

Note: It is very important that the jars aren't exposed to anything cold and that they have a natural and gradual cool-down. They can't touch countertops, metal racks—if the jars are exposed to a drastic temperature change, they may break. The last step (the cool-down process) will cause the vacuum seal to take place. Once the jars are cool, you will be able to check to see if the seal has set. Press down in the center. If it is down already, then the sealing process was successful and you can store the jars in a cool dark place for a year. If the seal did not set properly, store the jars in the refrigerator and eat the okra within several days. Once you open the seal, store the pickled product in the refrigerator, where it will keep for several months.

2½ cups white vinegar
½ cup granulated sugar
¼ cup sherry
2 tablespoons celery seeds
1 tablespoon chili powder
1 tablespoon salt

1 teaspoon Chili Paste (page 70), or 1 tablespoon cayenne pepper
1 bay leaf
2 cups fresh okra, rinsed

This is a really good way to enjoy okra. Not only is it great as a tabletop snack, but try cutting them up and throwing them into a salad—check out the response you get! Canning can sometimes be tricky, so if you are not completely sure about the process, please refer to *Stocking Up*, Vol. III, Carol Hupping (a Rodale Book), which includes detailed step-by-step illustrations and instructions.

* * *

Check your canning jars for any nicks or cracks, and make sure that the screw bands are not bent. Do not reuse flat lids. Wash the jars, lids, and bands with soap and warm water, and rinse well. Place the jars on a rack in a large pot. Fill the pot with water and boil for 15 minutes. Place the flat lids in a saucepan with water. Bring to a boil and remove from the heat. (In addition to sterilizing the lids, the hot water softens the rubber and helps create a tight seal.) Let the jars and lids stand in the hot water until you are ready to fill them.

In another pot, sterilize everything that is going to come in contact with the food, such as the stainless steel bowl, slotted spoons, and any other utensils you may need to use, by boiling them for 15 minutes.

In a large saucepan, combine the vinegar, sugar, sherry, celery seeds, chili powder, salt, Chili Paste, and bay leaf. Bring the mixture to a boil over high heat for a few minutes to dissolve the sugar and blend the ingredients. Add the okra and cook for 2 minutes (just enough to start the cooking process). Remove the pan from the heat.

Using a sterilized slotted spoon, place the okra in the jars. Check the flavor of the pickling solution, and correct it if necessary. Place the pan back on the heat and bring the mixture to a boil. Immediately fill all the jars to ¼ inch from the top. Wipe the jar rims and threads with a clean damp cloth. Cover quickly with the lids, and screw the bands on tight.

Place the jars back in the pot. Make sure they are covered by at least 2 inches of water. Boil the jars for 15 minutes. Remove the jars from the boiling water and place on several layers of folded paper towels or a wooden rack for the cool-down. This will take several hours.

Chili Paste

1 cups dried ancho chiles
½ cup warm water
4 to 5 fresh jalapeño peppers,
   stemmed

1½ to 2 cups fresh habanero or
   Scotch bonnet peppers,
   stemmed
¼ to ½ cup vegetable oil

I created this all-purpose flavoring mixture using three different types of chiles. The ancho is a smoked chile that registers around 6 or 7 on a heat scale of 1 to 10. Jalapeños rank about 5 or 6, and habaneros (or Scotch bonnets) are at 10. This paste has two purposes. One, of course, is to provide heat. The other is to add complexity to whatever you use it in because of the smoky flavor of the ancho chiles. I strongly suggest that you use this paste a little at a time and then taste the dish. Remember, you can always add more, but you can't take it away!

❊   ❊   ❊

First and most important, use gloves when you are working with the chiles.

Place the ancho chiles in the warm water and let stand for 15 minutes. Remove the chiles and drain off the excess water. Place the ancho chiles, jalapeños, and habaneros in the container of a blender. While adding the oil in a slow steady stream, process the peppers until a puree is formed. Store in a covered glass container in the refrigerator for up to 1 week.

Bread-n-Butter Pickle Mayonnaise

Makes about 2 cups

1 cup mayonnaise
½ cup finely chopped
  bread-and-butter pickles
1½ tablespoons fresh lemon
  juice
¼ teaspoon garlic powder
¼ teaspoon paprika
¼ teaspoon chili powder
¼ teaspoon cayenne pepper
Salt and freshly ground black
  pepper to taste

Use this as a spread for sandwiches, as a dip for chips, and even as a dressing for a salad. It's quick and easy to make and adds a lot of character to whatever dish you serve it with.

*   *   *

In a medium bowl, mix together all of the ingredients. Taste and check the seasoning, adding more salt and pepper if needed. Store in an airtight container in the refrigerator for up to 2 weeks.

Sweet Pickle Relish

¾ cup mayonnaise
½ cup finely chopped Pickled
   Okra (page 68)
¼ cup finely chopped
   bread-and-butter pickles
2 tablespoons grated onion
1 tablespoon fresh lemon juice

1 teaspoon celery seeds
¼ teaspoon chili powder
¼ teaspoon cayenne pepper
¼ teaspoon freshly ground black
   pepper
Salt to taste

This particular recipe calls for bread-and-butter pickles—unpeeled cucumber slices pickled with onion and sweet green bell peppers, and flavored with mustard, celery seeds, cloves, and turmeric. This relish brings character and versatility to the table, so I like to find interesting ways to use it. It is great with any fried fish dish.

❋ ❋ ❋

In a medium bowl, stir together all the ingredients except the salt until combined. Taste and check the seasoning, adding salt if needed. Store any leftovers in an airtight container in the refrigerator for up to 2 weeks.

Roasted Garlic and Garlic Oil

1 head garlic, separated into cloves and peeled

1 cup vegetable oil

Makes 1 cup garlic and oil

I love the taste of garlic, but sometimes I feel it can be overpowering. So to rectify that I make a batch of roasted garlic and roasted garlic oil. I use this in anything from mashed potatoes to coating meat, fish, or chicken. For coating, when the garlic is roasted and cooled down, I'll mash the garlic "meat" into a paste. Then I spread it onto my fish, for example, coat the fish with flour or bread crumbs, and pan-sear or sauté it. I often spread a little mashed garlic on bread or use it as a dip for chips. If you like garlic as much as I do, then I'm sure you will be able to come up with several other uses for this ingredient. I like to use the garlic oil as a base for salad dressings. I also use it as a bread dip by simply adding a few red pepper flakes and a touch of salt.

* * *

Preheat the oven to 350°F.

Place the garlic cloves and oil in a small ovenproof dish, and stir to coat. Cover and bake for 20 to 30 minutes, or until the garlic is soft and golden brown. Store together in an airtight container in the refrigerator for up to 4 weeks.

Roasted Shallots

10 shallots, broken into unpeeled cloves
2 tablespoons vegetable oil
¼ teaspoon salt
¼ teaspoon freshly ground black pepper

Make these flavorful shallots and keep them in a covered container in your refrigerator. Pureed, they make a delicious spread for sandwiches such as sliced pork or sliced steak. You can also use the puree in salad dressings. Basically the shallots can be used in anything that calls for onions. They will provide a milder, mellower flavor, perfect for when you want onion flavor but don't want it to overpower the dish.

❋   ❋   ❋

Preheat the oven to 350°F.

Place the shallots, oil, salt, and pepper in a small baking pan. Stir to coat the shallots with the oil and seasoning. Bake for about 20 minutes, shaking the pan occasionally, until the shallots are soft in the center. Store in an airtight container in the refrigerator for up to 1 week.

Chili Rub

½ cup corn, vegetable, or olive oil
1 teaspoon fresh lemon juice
1 teaspoon garlic powder
1 teaspoon freshly ground black pepper

1 teaspoon chili powder
1 teaspoon cayenne pepper
1 teaspoon crushed red pepper flakes
1 teaspoon ground cumin
1 teaspoon salt

Makes about 1 cup

Traditionally, African and Southern foods are spicy to very hot in their seasoning. The theory behind this is, when you live in a hot climate and you eat spicy foods, the weather will affect you less.

I use this rub as a marinade on beef, pork, and chicken. I prefer to put the rub on the night or even a whole day before to allow the seasoning to soak into the meat.

* * *

In a small bowl, stir together all the ingredients. Cover and refrigerate. Store in an airtight container in the refrigerator for up to 3 weeks.

Marv's Garlic Rub

Makes ½ cup

3 tablespoons garlic powder
2 tablespoons freshly ground
   black pepper
1 tablespoon onion powder

1 tablespoon dried thyme
1 tablespoon salt
1 teaspoon chili powder

This garlicky dry rub is really good on most meat dishes. For the best results, rub a little oil on the meat and then sprinkle the rub generously over both sides. Pan-sear the meat and then finish it for the required time in a preheated oven.

* * *

Mix all the ingredients thoroughly in a bowl. Store in an airtight container in a cool dark place. This is at its best within the first 6 months. After 6 months, dried spices tend to lose their intensity.

Blackened Red Pepper Spread

3 red bell peppers
½ cup mascarpone cheese (see Note)

¼ teaspoon fresh lemon juice
Salt and freshly ground black pepper to taste

Makes about ¾ cup

Note: Mascarpone is a creamy Italian cheese that is available at specialty food stores.

I'm not a big fan of mayonnaise, so I always try to come up with different types of flavorful spreads to dress sandwiches with. This can be used on meat, fish, vegetables, or poultry.

* * *

Preheat the broiler.

Position a broiler pan so that the tops of the peppers will be about 2 inches from the heat source. Roast the peppers for about 15 minutes, turning them about every 5 minutes, until the skins are blistered and charred all over. Transfer the peppers to a bowl, cover, and let steam until cooled.

Peel the blackened skins from the peppers. Cut each pepper into 3 large pieces. Remove the seeds and ribs.

Place the peppers in a blender or in a food processor fitted with the metal chopping blade, and process until almost smooth. Strain, and pour into a bowl. Add the cheese and lemon juice to the puree, and mix well. Taste and check the seasoning, adding salt and pepper if needed. Serve chilled. Store in an airtight container in the refrigerator for up to 7 days.

Pineapple and Cherry Chutney

Makes 3½ cups

2 cups dried Michigan (tart) cherries
2 tablespoons vegetable oil
1 medium onion, chopped
One 3-pound pineapple, peeled, cored, and cut into ½-inch pieces

2½ cups granulated sugar
1½ cups white balsamic vinegar, red balsamic vinegar, or red wine vinegar
¼ cup grated fresh ginger
¼ cup chopped fresh cilantro leaves

The pineapple is one fruit that I like to put in chutneys because it's so diverse. I like the texture—it won't break down and turn into mush if you cook it for a long period of time, so your chutney can have some crunch. Besides that, it brings a sweet-and-sour taste that a lot of chutneys require. So one day when I was looking to make a pork dish and I wanted to do something a little different to garnish the dish besides the normal apple or pear deal, I started playing around with pineapples and tart cherries, and I stumbled across this chutney. I might add that the stumbling-upon process is quite common in the kitchen, but it can be hit-or-miss. This happens to be a hit because it goes with pork, mild-flavored fish or chicken dishes, and even venison.

* * *

Place the cherries in a bowl and add enough hot tap water to cover. Cover the bowl and let stand for about 15 minutes to soften. Drain.

In a medium saucepan, heat the oil over medium heat. Add the onions and cook until softened, 3 to 5 minutes. Add the remaining ingredients and reduce the heat to low. Cook, stirring occasionally, until all the liquid is absorbed, about 2 hours. To cool the chutney quickly, pour the mixture out on a baking sheet. Once it is thoroughly cooled, place it in an airtight container and store it in the refrigerator for up to 3 months.

Tropical Fruit Chutney

2 tablespoons vegetable oil
½ onion, finely chopped
¼ cup minced fresh ginger
1½ cups chopped mango
½ cup chopped papaya
½ cup chopped pineapple
½ cup chopped guava
½ cup firmly packed light brown
  sugar
¼ cup granulated sugar

¾ cup champagne vinegar or
  white wine vinegar
1 fresh jalapeño pepper, stem
  removed, finely minced, with
  the seeds
One 3-inch cinnamon stick
1 teaspoon salt
1 teaspoon ground allspice
1 teaspoon ground coriander

Makes about 3¾ cups

Use this flavorful chutney to garnish a dessert or a spicy chicken dish. If you can't find the fresh varieties of these fruits, you can substitute canned or dried, adjusting the liquid accordingly.

* * *

In a large saucepan, heat the oil over medium heat. Add the onion and ginger and cook, stirring, until the onions are softened, 3 to 5 minutes. Add all the remaining ingredients and reduce the heat to low. Cook, stirring occasionally, until all the liquid is absorbed and the chutney is thick, 1½ to 2 hours. Remove from the stove and pour onto a flat tray. When the chutney is cooled, place it in an airtight container and store in the refrigerator for up to 3 months.

Sweet and Tart
Cherry Chutney

Makes 4 cups

2 tablespoons vegetable oil
½ small onion, finely diced
1 tablespoon finely minced fresh
  ginger
2½ cups dried Michigan (tart)
  cherries

1¼ cups dried Bing cherries
1¼ cups granulated sugar
⅓ cup raspberry vinegar
1 tablespoon fresh lemon juice
½ teaspoon salt

Basically cherries are either sweet or tart. Sweet cherries tend to be larger in size and can usually be eaten as is. Popular varieties include Bing, Lambert, and Tartarian. Tart cherries are smaller, and most of them are too sour to eat straight away. These cherries are great for pies, preserves, and chutneys. Early Richmond and Montmorency are common tart cherries. For this recipe, I have combined both types of cherries to create a sweet-and-sour balance in the chutney. I serve this with foie gras, duck, pork, and venison.

* * *

In a medium saucepan, heat the oil over medium heat. Add the onion and ginger and cook, stirring, until the onions are softened, 3 to 5 minutes. Add the remaining ingredients and reduce the heat to low. Cook, stirring occasionally, until all the liquid is absorbed, about 1½ hours. Store in an airtight container in the refrigerator. This chutney will keep for up to 3 months.

Asparagus and Summer Tomato Salad served with White Balsamic Vinaigrette

Pumpkin, Parsnip, and Butternut Squash Soup, served with Marv's Spiced Croutons

Black-Eyed Pea Cakes with Rutabaga Mash

Colombo-Dusted Sea Scallops with
Lentil Lima Bean Circuit Hash

Corn-Crusted
Porgies and
Five-Greens
Rice

Grilled Filet
Mignon with
Brown Oyster
Gravy, Yellow
Hominy Grits,
and Double-
Dipped Fried
Okra

Roast Pork Tenderloin with Brown Sugar Pineapple Jam, Yellow Hominy Grits, and Sweet Potato Muffin

Sweet Potato Crème Brûlée

Rice, Pilau, Starches, and Grains

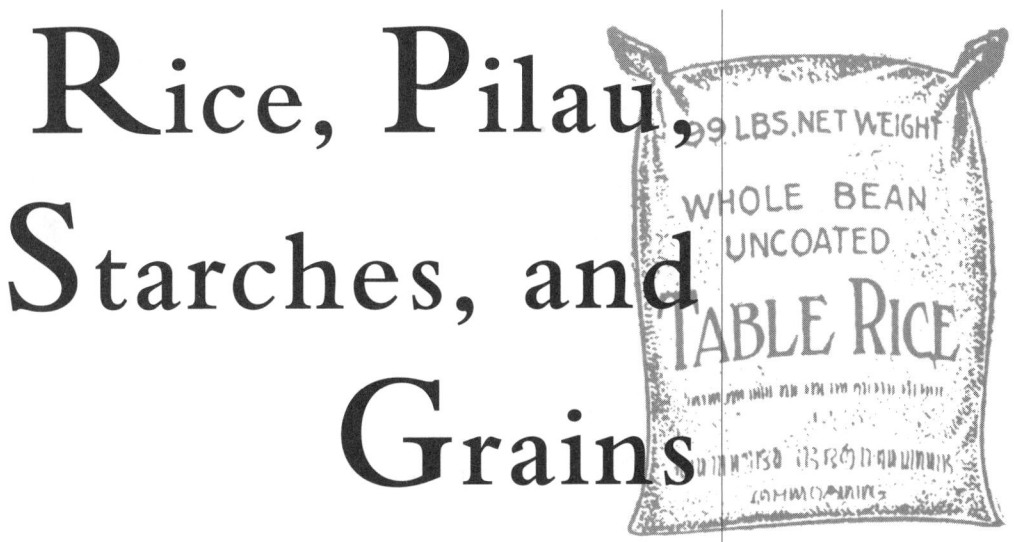

Rice is the primary staple of approximately two-thirds of the world's population, but in the United States its use is concentrated in the South. The crop was crucial to the economy of South Carolina. In fact, from the mid 1700s to the early 1800s South Carolina supplied 90 percent of the country's rice. The native strain, Carolina Gold, was considered the best in the world—so much so that it was exported to Europe during its heyday.

Although the famed Carolina Gold no longer exists, many more varieties of rice are available to today's cook, including brown, black, red, long, short, fluffy, and sticky. Avoid instant rices because you'll miss the nutty flavor and true texture.

White Rice

Makes 6 servings

3⅓ cups water
1½ cups uncooked long-grain
  white rice

¾ tablespoon salt

Cooking rice can be tricky sometimes. Since this book calls on rice often, I've included a basic rice recipe. This can be eaten quite simply as white rice, or you can prepare the rice ahead of time and use it for other dishes like Hoppin' John or pilau.

* * *

In a large saucepan, bring the water to a boil over high heat. Stir in the rice and salt. Cover and reduce the heat to medium-low. Simmer for 20 minutes. Remove from the heat. Let stand, covered, for 5 minutes or until the water is completely absorbed. Fluff with a fork.

Hoppin' John

3⅓ cups water
1½ cups uncooked white rice
¾ tablespoon salt
½ cup Creole Sauce (page 12)

¾ cup cooked Black-Eyed Peas
  (page 41)
Salt to taste

Makes 6 servings

There is much speculation as to how this dish got its name. We do know that it was approximately 1838 when it was first mentioned in print. The dish has a special purpose as well. African slaves and the Low-Country people believed that eating Hoppin' John on New Year's Day would bring good luck throughout the year because the beans resembled coins. That tradition still holds today. No matter who is writing the recipe or producing the dish, there are two basic ingredients: rice and peas. Traditionally cowpeas were used, but you can substitute black-eyed peas. This is a good accompaniment to gumbo.

❋   ❋   ❋

In a large saucepan, bring the water to a boil over high heat. Stir in the rice and salt. Cover and reduce the heat to medium-low. Simmer for 20 minutes. Remove from the heat. Let stand, covered, for 5 minutes or until the water is completely absorbed. Fluff with a fork. Leave the rice, covered, off to the side while preparing the rest of the dish.

In a medium saucepan, bring the Creole Sauce to a boil over low heat. Then add the black-eyed peas and cook until they are heated through, about 2 minutes. Place the cooked rice in a large bowl. Pour the sauce mixture into the bowl and combine thoroughly. Taste and check the seasoning, adding salt if needed. Transfer the Hoppin' John to a serving plate or bowl and eat it as is, or serve it with any type of gumbo or stew.

Crab and Shrimp Pilau

Makes 4 to 6 servings

1 teaspoon chili powder

1 teaspoon ground nutmeg

1 teaspoon cayenne pepper

1 teaspoon salt

1 teaspoon freshly ground black pepper

12 jumbo shrimp (1½ to 2 pounds), peeled and deveined

2 tablespoons vegetable oil, or more as needed

1 medium shallot, finely chopped

1 pound fresh okra, stems trimmed, cut into thin rounds

1 green bell pepper, seeded and diced

1 cup fresh or thawed frozen corn kernels

1 yellow onion, diced

2 cloves garlic, finely chopped

1 tablespoon finely chopped fresh sage leaves

1 tablespoon finely chopped fresh rosemary leaves, or ½ tablespoon dried

1 tablespoon finely chopped fresh thyme leaves, or ½ tablespoon dried

1 teaspoon celery seeds

4 ounces lump or jumbo lump crabmeat, flaked

2 to 2½ cups cooked White Rice (page 82)

1 medium tomato, peeled, seeded, and diced

Pilau is the Low-Country term for pilaf, a bulghur- or rice-based dish. To prepare pilau, you usually brown the ingredients in oil or butter before adding stock to finish the cooking. Once you understand the basic foundation of this dish, you can add or make changes to the ingredients. Instead of the crab and shrimp, you can use a whitefish like catfish or snapper. Chicken and/or sausage can be added too, with or without the fish.

To enhance the seafood flavor, serve the pilau with slices of lemon, and squeeze them over the dish just before eating.

* * *

In a medium bowl, mix together the chili powder, nutmeg, cayenne, salt, and black pepper. Add the shrimp and toss to coat with the seasoning mix.

In a large skillet, heat the oil over medium heat. Add the shrimp and cook about 1 minute on each side. Remove the shrimp and set aside. Add the shallots to the skillet, adding more oil if necessary. Cook, stirring, for 1 minute. Add the okra and bell pepper and stir. Cover, reduce the heat, and cook until the vegetables begin to soften slightly, about 5 minutes.

Add the corn, onions, garlic, sage, rosemary, thyme, and celery seeds to the skillet. Stir and cover. Cook until the onions are softened, about 5 minutes more. Increase the heat to medium-high and add the reserved shrimp and the crabmeat, stirring constantly for 1 minute. Stir in the rice and tomato and cook 2 to 3 minutes longer, or until heated through. Serve in a bowl or on plates.

Five-Greens Rice

Makes 8 servings

Mustard greens actually belong to the same family as broccoli, Brussels sprouts, kale, and kohlrabi. The leaves are very dark green in color and have a strong, bitter taste. They are available year-round in certain markets, being most abundant from December through early March. You can also buy them frozen or canned. When choosing fresh greens, look for firm medium-size leaves. Reject them if they have a yellowish color. When I use mustard greens, I usually mix them with other greens to cut the strong taste a bit.

3⅓ cups water
1½ cups uncooked long-grain white rice
¾ tablespoon salt
¼ cup flat parsley leaves
¼ pound chopped fresh spinach leaves
¼ pound chopped fresh mustard green leaves
¼ pound chopped fresh kale leaves
¼ cup chopped scallions, including the tender green tops
1 tablespoon vegetable, corn, or olive oil
Salt (optional)

Greens and rice are integral components of Southern cooking. In this recipe, an assortment of greens flavors the rice. It's a good side dish with meat, fish, and poultry.

* * *

In a large saucepan, bring the water to a boil over high heat. Stir in the rice and salt. Cover and reduce the heat to medium-low. Simmer for 20 minutes. Remove from the heat. Let stand, covered, for 5 minutes or until the water is completely absorbed. Fluff with a fork. Leave the rice, covered, off to the side while preparing the rest of the dish.

Bring a large saucepan of water to a boil. Add the parsley, spinach, mustard greens, kale, and scallions and blanch for 1 minute. Strain. Place the greens in an ice bath or under cold running water to stop the cooking process.

Strain the greens and place them in a blender or food processor. Process, using just enough water to puree the greens. Strain, saving 1 tablespoon of the liquid.

Heat a large skillet over medium heat. Add the oil, reserved tablespoon of liquid, and greens. Stir, and immediately add the cooked rice. Cook for 2 to 3 minutes, stirring constantly, until the rice is heated through. Taste and check the seasoning, adding salt if needed.

Brown Rice

1½ cups brown rice
2 tablespoons olive oil
¼ cup minced celery
1 clove garlic, minced

½ onion, minced
1 teaspoon Marv Spice
(page 64)

Makes 6 servings

Brown rice is light brown in color and has a nutty flavor with a chewy texture. It is processed by having only its outer husk removed. Brown rice contains bran, which limits its shelf life to about 6 months but also makes the rice more nutritious than White rice. Brown rice takes a little longer to cook than white rice (30 minutes), but there is a "quick" brown rice on the market that cooks in about 15 minutes. This rice goes well with anything you would serve white rice with.

* * *

Bring a large saucepan of water to a boil over medium heat. Add the rice. Reduce the heat and simmer for 30 to 40 minutes or until the rice is tender or soft. Drain off the water, and set the rice aside, covered, so it stays hot.

In a large saucepan, heat the oil over medium heat. Add the vegetables and cook, stirring, just until softened but not colored, 2 to 3 minutes. Add the Marv Spice and stir. Add the rice and stir. Transfer to serving bowls or plates.

Wild Rice

Makes 6 servings

4¾ cups Chicken Stock (page 6)
1½ cups wild rice
½ onion
1 carrot, cut in half crosswise
1 celery rib, cut in half crosswise
1 bay leaf
Pinch of salt

Wild rice has a distinctive nutty flavor and is chewy like brown rice. Technically this isn't a rice at all; it is defined as a long-grain marsh grass. Wild rice is native to the Great Lakes area, where it is harvested by the local Native Americans. When using wild rice, it is important to clean it thoroughly because it sometimes has a lot of debris mixed in with it. The best way to do this is to put the rice in a bowl, cover it with cold water, stir it with your hand, and let it sit for a couple of minutes. The debris is light and will float to the top. Allow yourself enough time when serving wild rice because the cooking process can take up to 1 hour.

* * *

Bring the stock to a boil in a large heavy-bottom saucepan over medium heat. Add the rice, vegetables, bay leaf, and salt. Stir well; then reduce the heat. Cover the saucepan and simmer until the rice begins to split open, 40 to 50 minutes. Drain, and remove the vegetables and bay leaf. Transfer the rice to serving dishes. Take care not to overcook the rice because it will become starchy.

Dirty Rice

2½ cups water
¼ teaspoon salt
2½ cups long-grain white rice
2 tablespoons vegetable oil
1 cup finely chopped red onion
2 cloves garlic, minced

2 cups chicken or turkey livers
1 tablespoon Marv Spice
  (page 64)
2¼ cups Chicken Stock
  (page 6)
1 bay leaf

Makes 6 servings

The name "dirty rice" comes from how the dish looks when it is presented—the ground-up chicken livers give the rice a dirty look. This dish is a Cajun staple. In addition to the livers, it may be made with bacon and/or green bell peppers.

❋ ❋ ❋

In a large saucepan, combine the water, salt, and rice and bring to a boil. Reduce the heat to low, cover, and simmer until the rice is tender, 10 to 12 minutes. Drain and rinse under hot running water to remove the excess starch. Place the rice back in the pan, off the heat, and cover to keep warm.

Heat the oil in a large heavy-bottom skillet over medium heat. Add the onion and garlic and cook, stirring continuously, until softened but not colored, about 5 minutes. Add the chicken livers and Marv Spice, and cook, stirring frequently, until the livers turn brown, about 8 minutes.

Pour the stock over the rice, set the pan over medium heat, and bring to a boil. Lower the heat and stir in the chicken liver mixture and bay leaf. Cook over low heat, stirring continuously, until the rice is soft and tender, 10 to 15 minutes.

Spiced Rice

Note: For best results, store spices in a cool, dry, dark place for up to 6 months.

2½ cups jasmine or other long-grain white rice
2 tablespoons vegetable oil
¼ cup minced onion
1 clove garlic, minced
1 teaspoon ground turmeric
1 teaspoon ground coriander
1 teaspoon ground cumin
1 teaspoon ground ginger

½ teaspoon ground nutmeg
½ teaspoon freshly ground black pepper
One 3-inch cinnamon stick
1 cup canned unsweetened coconut milk
1½ cups Chicken Stock (page 6)
1 bay leaf

Jasmine rice, an aromatic rice from Thailand, has a wonderful fragrance and goes well with fish or chicken dishes. Spices come from a variety of plant sources: stems, fruits, roots, and bark. At one time spices were valued so highly that they were used for trading, like currency. Spices have also been used for everything from medicinal purposes to dyeing cloth. Most people buy spices in the preground form because it is easy to use. For the most pungent flavor of a spice, buy it whole and grind a little when needed. You will taste a difference. If you do use whole spices, keep in mind that they are more intense in flavor than ground, so use them sparingly.

* * *

Place the rice in a bowl and fill the bowl with cool water. Pour off the water and repeat two or three more times, or until the water runs clear. Drain the rice. Heat the oil in a medium heavy-bottom saucepan over medium heat. Add the onion and garlic and cook, stirring continuously, until transparent but not colored, about 2 minutes. Add all the spices and stir. Add the rice, coconut milk, chicken stock, and bay leaf, and stir. Bring to a boil. Reduce the heat and simmer until all the liquid has been absorbed, about 10 minutes. Reduce the heat to very low, cover, and cook, stirring frequently so the rice doesn't stick to the bottom of the pan, for another 10 to 15 minutes. Serve hot.

Coconut Rice

2½ cups jasmine or other long-grain white rice
1 tablespoon vegetable oil
2 teaspoons minced fresh ginger
1½ cups canned unsweetened coconut milk

1½ cups water
One ½-inch cinnamon stick
Pinch of salt
½ cup minced fresh cilantro
2 scallions, white and light green parts finely chopped

Coconuts, said to have originated in Malaysia, now grow in most tropical areas around the world. In some cases you will find influences of the Caribbean in Low-Country cooking, and this is one of those examples. Because we are using unsweetened coconut the flavor is subtle, but it gives the rice a pleasant perfume-like quality.

Canned coconut milk is available in most supermarkets.

* * *

Place the rice in a bowl and fill the bowl with cold water. Pour off the water and repeat this procedure three times or until the water runs clear. Drain the rice.

Heat the oil in a medium heavy-bottom saucepan over medium heat. Add the ginger and cook, stirring continuously, for 1 minute. Add the rice and stir. Cook for 3 minutes, stirring continuously. Add the coconut milk, water, cinnamon stick, and salt, and stir. Bring to a boil, then reduce the heat and simmer until the rice has absorbed all of the liquid, about 10 minutes; stir frequently to prevent the rice from sticking to the bottom. Cover, reduce the heat to very low, and cook until rice is soft and tender, 10 to 15 minutes more. Stir in the cilantro and scallions. Transfer to a serving dish or individual plates.

Golden Rice

Makes 6 to 8 servings

1 tablespoon vegetable oil
½ onion, finely diced
1 teaspoon saffron threads
1 teaspoon ground turmeric
2 cups uncooked long-grain
   white rice

2¼ cups water
1 bay leaf
¾ tablespoon salt

In the late 1600s and through most of the 1700s, when the rice business was flourishing in the Low Country, the rice was called "golden rice." It was said if you looked out across a field of this rice, it looked like a sea of gold. Now golden rice is pretty much lost—you can't find it commercially any more. The saffron in this recipe gives the rice a rich golden color and gives off a sweet floral aroma that just makes everything it is paired with taste better. Golden Rice goes really well with most fish and chicken dishes.

❋   ❋   ❋

In a large saucepan, heat the oil over medium-high heat. Add the onion and cook, stirring, until transparent, 5 to 7 minutes. Add the saffron, turmeric, and rice and stir together for 1 minute. Add the water, bay leaf, and salt, and bring the mixture to a boil. Stir with a fork to prevent the mixture from clumping. Cover and reduce the heat. Simmer until the grains of rice are tender, about 15 minutes.

Yellow Hominy Grits

1 tablespoon vegetable oil
1 white onion (preferably Vidalia), grated
½ cup fresh or thawed frozen corn kernels
1 cup milk
1 cup water

1 cup yellow grits or coarse-ground yellow cornmeal
2 tablespoons unsalted butter
1 teaspoon salt
1 teaspoon freshly ground black pepper

Makes 6 servings

Grits are grains that have been dried and ground. The most common grits are corn (hominy), but there are oat and rice grits too. Grits come in fine, medium, and coarse grinds. Yellow hominy grits are available in specialty stores or by mail order.

Hominy is dried hulled corn kernels, and grits are a finer-ground version. Both are prepared in a variety of ways and are a staple in the South. They are used in breakfast dishes, frequently served with butter and sugar, as well as being used in savory side dishes and main courses. Here's a side dish that is a nice change of pace from rice or potatoes. I like to serve grits with anything from bacon and eggs for breakfast to shrimp, salmon, or a spicy piece of chicken for dinner. *Note:* The same product that Italians use for polenta, cornmeal, can be used for grits.

❋ ❋ ❋

In a medium saucepan, heat the oil over medium heat. Add the onion and cook, stirring, until transparent, about 2 minutes. Add the corn and cook, stirring occasionally, or until the kernels become soft, about 5 minutes. Add the milk and water and bring the mixture to a boil. Whisk in the grits, reduce the heat to low, and simmer, stirring constantly, until the grits become thick, about 30 minutes. Stir in the butter, salt, and pepper.

Macaroni and Cheese

Makes 4 to 6 servings

¾ cup heavy cream
¼ cup shredded Swiss cheese
¼ cup shredded mild cheddar
  cheese
1 pound elbow macaroni,
  cooked according to the
  package directions

1½ teaspoons Marv Spice
  (page 64)

If you are trying to cut calories and fat, you might want to bypass this recipe. Some things just aren't right without cream and cheese, and folks, this is one of them.

Macaroni has been enjoyed by the English since at least the 16th century. In England, as in Italy, it was consumed with different types of sauces, frequently tomato. In 1937 Kraft Foods introduced the "Kraft Dinner," which featured macaroni and cheese. This became a big hit in the United States and especially in the South. Here is my made-from-scratch interpretation.

* * *

Preheat the oven to 350°F.

In a medium saucepan, bring the cream to a boil over medium heat and cook until it starts to thicken, about 5 minutes. Add half of the Swiss cheese and half of the cheddar cheese and stir to melt. Add the cooked macaroni and the Marv Spice, and cook for 2 minutes, stirring occasionally. Scrape the mixture into a 9-inch square baking dish. Cover with the remaining cheeses, and bake for 5 to 7 minutes or until the cheese on top has completely melted.

Couscous

1½ cups Chicken Stock
  (page 6) or water
1½ cups couscous
1 tablespoon olive oil
1 tablespoon unsalted butter

¼ cup coarsely chopped unsalted
  pistachios or slivered almonds
¼ cup raisins (optional)

Makes 6 servings

To some people couscous is a mystery, and they don't use it enough. It is a staple in North African cuisine, and it's so versatile that it can be served for breakfast, as a salad, or mixed with nuts for a final course. You can find it at your local supermarket and prepare it in 10 minutes. Couscous is traditionally served with lamb and chicken, but you can use it as a starch for any meal.

* * *

Bring the stock to a boil in a small saucepan.

Place the couscous in a medium bowl. Add the oil and butter to the boiling stock, pour the hot mixture over the couscous, and stir. Cover tightly with plastic wrap so no air escapes. Set aside to rest for 5 minutes.

Remove the plastic wrap. Using a fork, scrape the top of the couscous until some of it comes loose, and transfer the loosened couscous to another bowl. Repeat this operation until all the couscous is in the bowl. Toss in the nuts and the raisins, if using. Serve immediately, or cool and serve at room temperature.

Peach Tea Couscous

Makes 4 to 6 servings

2 peach-flavored tea bags
1 cup boiling water
One 10-ounce box couscous
1 tablespoon unsalted butter

¼ teaspoon salt
¼ teaspoon freshly ground black
  pepper

Couscous, which originated in North Africa, is actually semolina pasta. Semolina is a coarse grind of durum wheat, not a flour or a type of wheat. The beauty of this product is the diversity of it. I use it in breakfast dishes, salads, and as a starch with main courses. Peach-flavored tea bags add a Southern touch to this basic recipe. This side dish goes nicely with spicy chicken or grilled fish.

* * *

Place the tea bags in the boiling water and let steep for 3 minutes. Put the couscous in a medium bowl. Add the butter, salt, and pepper to the couscous. Remove the tea bags from the water and pour the water over the couscous. Cover the bowl with plastic wrap and let sit for 10 minutes. Remove the plastic wrap. Using the tines of a fork, fluff the couscous.

Vegetables, Mash, and Circuit Hash

The South is home to a host of vegetables: Savoy cabbage, Brussels sprouts, asparagus, beets, broccoli, eggplant, summer and winter squash, spinach, sorrel, mushrooms, sweet potatoes, pumpkins, sea kale, celery, cauliflower, and "tomatas."

A "mash" is a pureed vegetable—potatoes, rutabagas, carrots, turnips, as well as all manner of squash. Root vegetables were an African staple. Get inspired to do the mash with the recipes that begin on page 111.

"Circuit hash" is a corruption of the word succotash. The traditional succotash might consist of lima beans, corn, and a little cream or milk. Never one to be satisfied with bland food, Low-Country cooks dress up a succotash with tomatoes, red peppers, and a combination of fava, pole, and green beans cooked in a fresh vegetable stock. Voilà!—circuit hash. Makes your mouth water, doesn't it?

One last word about vegetables: okra. Most Southerners just can't get enough of the versatile pod, be it fried with cornmeal to a delicious crunch, pickled as a tart relish, steamed as a delicate side dish, or served as a garnish in a salad. Much maligned as slimy—by people who don't know how to cook it—okra becomes sublime in the hands of a Low-Country cook.

Sautéed Collard Greens

Makes 6 servings

3 pounds collard greens
3 tablespoons vegetable oil
1 carrot, chopped
½ onion, chopped
2 teaspoons finely chopped fresh
thyme leaves, or 1 teaspoon
dried
2 teaspoons finely chopped fresh
sage leaves, or 1 teaspoon
dried
2 teaspoons finely chopped fresh
rosemary leaves, or 1 teaspoon
dried

1½ cups Vegetable Stock
(page 8)
¼ cup white balsamic vinegar or
white wine vinegar
Tabasco or other hot pepper
sauce to taste
Salt and freshly ground black
pepper to taste

Collard greens are a staple of the South, where they were substituted for a similar green used in Africa. These greens are the type of dish that can cause "much ado about nothing" because so many people feel that there is only one true way to prepare them: that is, to cook them all day long with salt pork, fatback, or a ham hock. Personally and professionally, I don't believe in that method. I believe that cooking a vegetable for so long ruins it. Besides that, you lose all of the nutrients and the natural texture. Some of you won't agree with this, and I understand that too. But think about this: I love to challenge myself and others when it comes to classic dishes. They may have been prepared in such a way some time ago, which was right for that time but maybe not so right for this time. I'm not trying to reinvent the wheel here, I'm just making a few adjustments that may benefit people who have dietary restraints or are concerned about what they eat. This is not low-fat food, just fat-conscious. If you try these greens with an open mind, you will be hooked.

* * *

Cut the bottoms off the collard greens and place the leaves in a sink full of cold water. Swish them around and let the dirt fall to the bottom. Remove the greens from the water, drain and refill the sink, and repeat the procedure. When the greens are clean, use the point of a sharp knife to trim along both sides of the center vein on each leaf and remove it. Cut the leaves into 1-inch pieces.

In a large saucepan, heat the oil over medium heat. When the oil is hot, add the carrot and onion and cook, stirring, until the vegetables are softened, about 5 minutes. Add the herbs and cook, stirring constantly, for 30 seconds to allow the flavors to blend. Add the greens, stir, cover, and cook for 2 minutes. Add the stock, vinegar, Tabasco, and salt and pepper to taste. Cover and reduce the heat to low. Cook for 30 to 40 minutes, or longer if you like your greens to be softer.

Roasted Corn

Makes 8 servings

8 ears corn, in their husks

2 tablespoons corn oil

I like to use roasted corn kernels in different dishes. Roasting tones down the flavor and makes it more subtle.

* * *

Preheat the oven to 350°F.

Soak the ears of corn in water to cover for 15 minutes. Remove the ears from the water and place them on a baking sheet. Using your hands, rub the oil over the husks. Bake for 40 minutes. Remove from the oven and serve. If you are using just the kernels, let the roasted ears cool. Remove the husks and silk from each ear. Stand each ear of corn upright and using a sharp knife, cut down along the sides to remove the kernels of corn.

Baby Green Beans

1½ to 2 pounds fresh haricots verts (baby green beans)
2 tablespoons vegetable, corn, or olive oil

2 tablespoons minced shallots
1 tablespoon minced garlic

Makes 4 to 6 servings

I like the thinner green beans. They have the flavor, but it's subtle. The texture is also delicate. It's easy to successfully pair these with a variety of foods.

* * *

Bring a large saucepan of water to a boil. Add the haricots verts and blanch for 2 minutes. Drain. (If you are not using the haricots verts right away, place them in ice-cold water to stop the cooking process.)

In a large skillet, heat the oil over medium-high heat. Add the shallots and garlic and cook, stirring, until softened, 2 to 3 minutes. Add the blanched haricots verts and toss to coat with the mixture. Cook until heated through, about 1 minute longer.

Stewed Okra

3 tablespoons vegetable oil
1 small onion or 1 shallot, finely chopped
1 tablespoon finely chopped garlic
2 pounds fresh okra, cut into ½-inch-thick slices
1 cup fresh or thawed frozen corn kernels

1½ cups peeled whole tomatoes, undrained, chopped
2 tablespoons finely chopped fresh thyme leaves, or 1 tablespoon dried
4 cups Vegetable Stock (page 8)
Salt and freshly ground black pepper to taste

People either hate okra or they love it. I was exposed to okra at a young age because my mother loved it. I didn't. Now I've grown to appreciate it and I use it in a lot of different ways, such as for pickling, stewing, and frying.

* * *

In a large saucepan, heat the oil over medium heat. Add the onion and garlic and cook, stirring, until softened, about 2 minutes. Stir in the okra and the corn. Cook, stirring constantly, reducing the heat if necessary, until the okra is tender, about 5 minutes.

Stir in the tomatoes and thyme and let the mixture come to a slow boil. Add the stock and bring back to a slow boil. Then reduce the heat and simmer for 20 minutes. Check the seasoning, adding salt and pepper if needed.

Cooked Lentils

1 teaspoon vegetable oil
¼ cup finely diced smoked
   bacon (optional)
1 celery rib, finely diced
1 carrot, finely diced
½ shallot, finely diced
½ cup dry red wine
½ cup red wine vinegar
2 tablespoons granulated sugar
3 cups Chicken Stock or
   Vegetable Stock
   (page 6 or 8)

1½ cups *du Puy* lentils
   (see Note, page 104)
1 bay leaf
2 sprigs fresh thyme, or
   1 teaspoon dried
1 tablespoon salt
1 tablespoon freshly ground
   black pepper

Makes 3 cups, or
6 servings

There are three basic types of lentils: brownish green, reddish orange, and the French variety, which is tiny and dark green. These are known as *lentilles du Puy*, and they are the lentils I like to use. They have good flavor but the texture is delicate and subtle. Lentils are good as a side dish with most meat, fish, and poultry dishes.

* * *

In a medium saucepan, heat the oil over medium heat. Add the bacon, if using, and cook until it starts to brown, 4 to 5 minutes. Add the celery, carrot, and shallot and cook, stirring, until they start to soften, about 5 minutes. Pour off any excess fat. Add the red wine, vinegar, and sugar and cook to reduce the liquid by half, 5 to 7 minutes. Add the stock and lentils and bring the mixture to a simmer. Add the bay leaf, thyme, salt, and pepper. Check the seasoning and adjust if necessary. Cover and cook over low heat until the lentils are al dente, about 35 minutes. Remove the bay leaf and thyme sprigs before serving.

Lentil Lima Bean Circuit Hash

Makes 6 servings

Note: *Du Puy* lentils are smaller than the supermarket variety. They are available at specialty foods stores. I like working with the *du Puy* variety, but if they are unavailable, you can substitute regular lentils.

1 cup dried *du Puy* lentils (see Note)
2 tablespoons vegetable oil
1 shallot, finely chopped
1 teaspoon finely chopped fresh thyme leaves, or ½ teaspoon dried
¼ cup corn kernels (preferably fresh)
¼ cup cooked or thawed frozen lima beans
¼ cup tiny cherry tomatoes, such as teardrop or currant tomatoes, cut in half
2 cups Chicken Stock or Vegetable Stock (page 6 or 8)
1 tablespoon unsalted butter
Salt and freshly ground black pepper to taste

Circuit hash and succotash are basically one and the same. You can't make either without lima beans and corn. Depending on the recipe you are following, cream or stock may be used to finish the recipe. The beauty of a succotash like this is that it serves a multitude of purposes. It can be served as a vegetable dish or as a sauce for poultry or meat. Sometimes I take a nice piece of fish and sear it on both sides. Then I place the fish in the same pan as the cooked succotash and finish it in the oven.

* * *

Rinse the lentils well under running water, discarding any small stones or debris. Place the lentils in a medium saucepan and add enough water to cover them by an inch or two. Bring to a boil over high heat. Reduce the heat to low. Simmer, partially covered, until the lentils are tender but not mushy, 18 to 20 minutes. Do not overcook. Drain immediately.

Heat the oil in a medium saucepan over moderate heat. Add the shallot and cook, stirring, until slightly softened, about 2 minutes. Add the thyme and stir. Add the corn, lima beans, and tomatoes. Cook together, stirring occasionally, to blend the flavors, 3 to 4 minutes. Add the cooked lentils and the stock. Bring the mixture to a simmer and cook for 5 minutes, reducing the liquid slightly. Stir in the butter. Taste and check the seasoning, adding salt and pepper if needed.

Currant tomatoes are the tiniest tomatoes you can find. They come in both red and yellow and produce an amazing tomato flavor. They can be found in most gourmet shops.

Teardrop tomatoes are a little larger—but smaller than cherry tomatoes—and also have a lot of flavor.

Butternut Squash Succotash

Makes 4 to 5 servings

1 tablespoon vegetable oil
1 butternut squash (1½ to 2 pounds), peeled, seeded, and cut into ¼-inch dice
½ green bell pepper, seeded and chopped
½ red bell pepper, seeded and chopped
½ shallot, minced
½ cup fresh or thawed frozen corn kernels
¼ cup thawed frozen lima beans
¾ cup cooked or canned black beans, drained
¾ cup Vegetable Stock (page 8)
1 tablespoon finely chopped fresh thyme leaves, or
½ tablespoon dried
1 tablespoon finely chopped fresh sage leaves, or
½ tablespoon dried
1 tablespoon finely chopped fresh rosemary leaves, or
½ tablespoon dried
Salt and freshly ground black pepper to taste
1 tablespoon unsalted butter (optional)

Succotash is boiled corn kernels. The word comes from the Narragansett Indian word *msickquatash*. In the South, succotash usually involves lima beans as well. In this recipe, I have added butternut squash and black beans to create a dish that looks great. I like to work with butternut squash because of its firm texture and subtle sweet taste. This dish works really well with most fish dishes and a side of rice. Roast chicken will serve up nicely with this too.

❋   ❋   ❋

In a saucepan, heat the oil over medium heat. Add the squash, bell peppers, and shallot and cook, stirring, until the squash starts to soften, 3 to 4 minutes. Add the corn and both beans and cook, stirring, 1 minute longer. Add the stock. Reduce the heat to low and simmer for 5 minutes to reduce the liquid. Add the herbs and salt and pepper to taste. Stir in the butter, if desired.

Southern Summer Ratatouille

3 tablespoons vegetable oil
½ onion, finely diced
1 tablespoon finely chopped
   fresh garlic
1½ teaspoons grated fresh ginger
1 red bell pepper, seeded and
   finely diced
1 green bell pepper, seeded and
   finely diced
½ cup fresh or thawed frozen
   corn kernels

1 cup diced unpeeled eggplant
1 cup sliced fresh okra
½ cup diced unpeeled zucchini,
   outer part only, seeds discarded
1 cup chopped canned peeled
   plum tomatoes
1 tablespoon chopped fresh
   thyme leaves, or ½ tablespoon
   dried
Salt and freshly ground black
   pepper to taste

Makes 6 to 8 servings

Basically it is a dish from Provence that is prepared with tomato, eggplant, peppers, garlic, and zucchini as the base. In ours we add a few Southern staples to give it that Low-Country flavor. This dish can be used as an accompaniment or as a vegetable dish that stands on its own. It can be served hot or cold.

*　*　*

Heat the oil in large sauté pan over medium heat. Add the onion and garlic and cook, stirring occasionally, until the onions become soft, about 2 minutes. Reduce the heat to medium-low. Add the ginger and bell peppers and cook until the peppers become soft, 3 to 5 minutes. Add the corn, eggplant, and okra, cover the pan, and lower the heat so the vegetables can simmer until the okra is soft, 5 to 7 minutes. Add the zucchini, tomatoes, and thyme, place the cover back on, and allow to simmer for another 5 minutes. Check the seasoning, adding salt and pepper if needed.

Baked Sweet Potatoes

Makes 4 to 6 servings

4 to 6 sweet potatoes, scrubbed
1 tablespoon vegetable, corn, or
  olive oil

Among Southerners, sweet potatoes are a favorite whether they are used in a puree, soup, or pie or simply baked. (See also my recipe for Sweet Potato Crème Brûlée on page 182.) Native Americans were already growing sweet potatoes when Columbus arrived in 1492. In the South, they were frequently used by the African slaves. They used this vegetable interchangeably with the yam, which is indigenous to Africa and some Latin American countries. Even though the yam and the sweet potato are still used interchangeably today, they come from two different plants. Similar in size and shape, yams contain a higher moisture and sugar content than sweet potatoes. Sweet potatoes are grown in this country, whereas yams aren't. Sweet potatoes are often called yams in recipes. In fact, canned sweet potatoes are usually labeled as yams or candied yams. (Go figure!) All I know is that if a recipe calls for sweet potatoes or yams, you can use either of the two and it will come out just fine.

* * *

Preheat the oven to 350°F.

Rub the sweet potatoes with the oil. Place them on a baking sheet and bake for 45 to 60 minutes, or until they give when lightly squeezed. Serve hot out of the oven, with butter, or let cool for another use.

Lemony Sweet Potato Puree

8 sweet potatoes (about 2½ pounds)
¾ cup firmly packed light brown sugar
½ cup (1 stick) unsalted butter
2 large eggs
1 teaspoon ground cinnamon
1 teaspoon ground nutmeg
½ cup fresh lemon juice
1 tablespoon vanilla extract
Salt and freshly ground black pepper to taste

Makes 8 to 10 servings

Candied yams are an important part of any real Southern meal. This recipe is my take on the classic. True yams are indigenous to Africa. When the African slaves arrived in the New World, they made use of the sweet potatoes that were available here.

* * *

Preheat the oven to 350°F.

Place the potatoes on a baking sheet and bake for 45 to 60 minutes, or until they give when lightly squeezed. Remove the potatoes from the oven and let cool. Check occasionally to see when the potatoes are cool enough for you to remove the skins (the skins are easier to remove when the potatoes are still fairly warm).

Place the peeled sweet potatoes in the container of a food processor fitted with the metal chopping blade (you can also beat the potatoes using an electric mixer). Add the remaining ingredients except the salt and pepper and process until combined. Scrape the mixture into a medium-size baking dish and bake in the oven for about 8 to 10 minutes, or until the mixture registers 160°F. Taste and check the seasoning, adding salt and pepper if needed.

Sweet Potato Fries

½ teaspoon ground nutmeg
½ teaspoon chili powder
½ teaspoon cayenne pepper
½ teaspoon celery salt
¼ teaspoon ground coriander
¼ teaspoon ground cumin

Vegetable oil for deep frying
6 sweet potatoes, cut into
  julienne strips

Simple to make, these are a nice change of pace from ordinary French fries. I serve these fries with steak or pork chops, but they work well with most anything that you would ordinarily serve with French fries. Try sprinkling them with Marv Spice (page 64) or dunking them in Marv's Hot Sauce (page 67) or another favorite hot sauce.

* * *

In a small bowl, stir together the nutmeg, chili powder, cayenne, celery salt, coriander, and cumin.

In a deep fryer or a large deep skillet, heat the oil over medium-high heat until it registers 375°F on a deep-fat thermometer. Add the sweet potato strips and cook until crispy and golden, 5 to 7 minutes. Using a slotted spoon, transfer the cooked sweet potatoes to several layers of paper towels to drain. Sprinkle with the spice mixture.

Rutabaga Carrot Mash

3 to 4 rutabagas, peeled and
  coarsely chopped
1 Vidalia onion, cut in half
Salt to taste

4 carrots, coarsely chopped
½ cup (1 stick) unsalted butter
Freshly ground black pepper to
  taste

Makes 6 to 8 servings

Rutabagas are believed to be a hybrid of turnips and cabbage and to have originated in Russia only about 250 years ago. They are also known as Swedes or Swedish turnips. They are available year-round, but their peak is in the fall. Rutabagas are frequently coated with wax before they are shipped so they will hold up better. As with other root vegetables, when cooked, the rutabaga has a slightly sweet taste. It pairs beautifully with other vegetables. Look for rutabagas that are smooth, firm, and heavy for their size. And if they are coated with wax, make sure to use a very sharp knife and cut carefully!

* * *

Place the rutabagas and one of the onion halves in a large saucepan. Add water to cover, and salt the water. Bring the mixture to a boil over medium heat. Reduce the heat and simmer until the rutabagas are tender when pierced with the point of a sharp knife, about 35 minutes. Drain.

Meanwhile, place the carrots and remaining onion half in another large saucepan. Add water to cover and salt the water. Bring the mixture to a boil over medium heat. Reduce the heat and simmer until the carrots are tender when pierced with the point of a sharp knife, about 20 minutes. Drain.

Place the rutabagas, carrots, and onions in a food processor fitted with the metal chopping blade, or in a blender. Process just until the mixture is smooth. Add the butter and process to combine. Taste and check the seasoning, adding salt and pepper if needed.

Celeriac Puree

Makes 4 to 6 servings

3 celeriac bulbs, pared and
coarsely chopped
1 Vidalia onion, coarsely
chopped
Salt

3 potatoes, coarsely chopped
½ cup (1 stick) unsalted butter
Freshly ground black pepper to
taste

Celeriac, also known as celery root or celery knob, is a root vegetable that can be eaten cooked or raw. The flavor is of celery but the texture is more like a combination of potato and water chestnut. The root is white to beige in color and is kind of knobby. Celeriac is in abundance between September and May.

* * *

Place the celeriac and half of the onions in a medium saucepan. Add water to cover, and salt the water. Bring the mixture to a boil over medium heat. Reduce the heat and simmer until the celeriac is tender when pierced with the point of a sharp knife, about 25 minutes.

Meanwhile, in another saucepan, combine the potatoes, the remaining onions, and salted water to cover. Bring the mixture to a boil over medium heat. Reduce the heat and simmer until the potatoes are tender, about 20 minutes.

Drain all of the vegetables and place them in a ricer and process until smooth. Add the butter and process to combine. Taste and check the seasoning, adding salt and pepper if needed.

Parsnip Mash

2 pounds parsnips, cut into
  1-inch pieces
1½ pounds Idaho potatoes, cut
  into 1-inch pieces
¼ cup (½ stick) unsalted butter

Salt and freshly ground black
  pepper to taste (use white
  pepper if you don't want it to
  show)

Makes 6 to 8 servings

It's thought that parsnips were brought to the United States by Europeans in the early 1600s. Available all year round, they are at their peak in the fall and winter. Parsnips have a carrot-like shape but they are a beige color. When buying, look for small to medium well-shaped roots that are not limp or spotted. Parsnips have a versatile flavor and work well with most meat, chicken, and fish dishes.

* * *

Cook the parsnips and the potatoes in separate pots of boiling salted water until the vegetables are soft enough for mashing, 20 to 30 minutes. Strain, and place the parsnips and potatoes in a food processor fitted with the metal chopping blade, or in a ricer. Process until pureed. Add the butter and mix thoroughly. Taste and check the seasoning, adding salt and pepper if needed.

Gems from the Sea

Low-Country cookery is a cuisine of the water, born of the ocean and the freshwater marshes, ponds, rivers, and tributaries that hug the flat coastal tideland of South Carolina and parts of Georgia. The African influence is deliciously evident here. Slaves were inventive with the local cornucopia—crabs, clams, oysters, shrimp, mackerel, bass, flounder, grouper, catfish, turtle, eel, and crayfish. From their own tradition they introduced slow stewpot cooking using such ingredients as hot peppers, okra, eggplant, collards, and peanuts.

Southern seafood dishes are among the most sophisticated because of their complex layers of flavors. They unfold on the palate like a robust red wine. What's more, because of the abundance of spices and flavors, they can be made on the light side, with little fat.

Salmon Cakes

Makes 8 cakes, or
4 servings

2½ cups milk
8 sprigs cilantro
Salt
1 pound boneless salmon fillet,
cut into 1-inch pieces
½ pound sliced white bread,
crusts removed
3 tablespoons plus ½ cup
vegetable, corn, or olive oil
1 red bell pepper, seeded and
finely chopped

1 green bell pepper, seeded and
finely chopped
½ onion, finely chopped
2 celery ribs, finely chopped
2 tablespoons Marv Spice
(page 64)
2 tablespoons Marv's Bay Spice
(page 66)
6 large egg whites
2½ cups dried bread crumbs
(such as Japanese *panko*)

The secret to this recipe is using fresh bread, not dried bread crumbs, which tend to be overwhelming in many cake and croquette recipes. This enables you to get the true flavor of the other ingredients. I use dried bread crumbs just to lightly coat the outside of the cakes. The Blackened Red Pepper Spread (page 77), the Dill Lemon Dressing (page 128), and the Bread-n-Butter Pickle Mayonnaise (page 71) accompany these cakes well.

* * *

In a medium saucepan, heat the milk, cilantro, and a pinch of salt over high heat until it boils. Reduce the heat to low and add the salmon. Simmer until the salmon is cooked, 7 to 10 minutes. Remove the salmon with a slotted spoon and set it aside to cool.

Add the bread, one piece at a time, to the milk. When it has soaked up as much milk as possible, use a slotted spatula to transfer the bread to a colander to drain and cool.

In a large skillet, heat the 3 tablespoons oil over medium-high heat. Add the bell peppers, onion, and celery, and cook, stirring, until slightly softened, about 5 minutes. Transfer the vegetable mixture to a large bowl. Add the salmon and break it into small pieces. Add the soaked bread, Marv Spice, and Marv's Bay Spice, and mix well, breaking up the bread. Taste and check the seasoning, adding salt if needed.

Pinch off a 2-inch ball of the salmon mixture and form it into a cake shape. Repeat this procedure until all of the mixture is used. Place the egg whites in a shallow dish and lightly beat. Place the dried bread crumbs in a separate shallow dish or bowl. Dip each cake first in the egg whites and then in the bread crumbs so that they are all coated.

Preheat the oven to 350°F.

In a large skillet, heat the remaining ½ cup oil over medium-high heat. Dip the edge of one of the cakes into the oil to detect when it is hot or check the temperature by using a fry thermometer at 350° (the edge of the cake should sizzle). Place a few cakes in the oil and cook until golden brown on the bottom, 2 to 3 minutes. Turn and cook the other side, 2 to 3 minutes more. Using a slotted spatula, transfer the cooked cakes to several layers of paper towels to drain. Repeat the procedure until all the cakes are browned. Place the cakes on a baking sheet and bake in the oven for 5 to 7 minutes, or until they are hot in the center. (Check by sticking the tip of a knife into the center of one cake.)

Corn-Crusted Porgies

Makes 4 servings

Note: One tablespoon of Marv Spice (page 64) can be substituted for the celery salt, chili powder, and black and cayenne peppers in the marinade.

For the marinade
1½ cups buttermilk
1 teaspoon celery salt
½ teaspoon chili powder
¼ teaspoon freshly ground black pepper
¼ teaspoon cayenne pepper
2½ pounds boned porgy fillets

For the cornmeal crust
½ cup all-purpose flour
½ cup fine yellow cornmeal
¼ teaspoon salt
¼ teaspoon freshly ground black pepper

Vegetable oil

Here is one of my favorite recipes. It tastes great and it reminds me of my dad, who is a big fan of this fish. (He also taught me how to cook when I was seven years old. Dad wanted me to be self-sufficient.)

The porgy is a white-fleshed fish with a sweet flavor. It is sometimes used in place of snapper. The name of this Southern delicacy comes from the Narragansett Indian word mishcuppauog, which can be shortened to pauog, porgy, or scup. A native of North Carolina, my dad grew up eating this economical fish—and so did I. As a chef at a New York City restaurant, I once featured porgies as a special. I believe I fetched twenty-something bucks for that dish, and people loved it. I gave my dad a call and told him that I ran his fish as a special and told him the NYC price. He laughed and volunteered to drive up from North Carolina the next day with a truckload full of porgies. A close cousin to the porgy is the sea bream, which can be substituted in this recipe.

The acid in the buttermilk breaks down the sinew in the fish, allowing the spices to penetrate into the flesh as well as making the texture of the fish softer.

* * *

In a large bowl, whisk together all the marinade ingredients. Place the porgy fillets in the mixture and gently toss to coat with the marinade. Refrigerate for at least 4 hours and up to 12 hours. (If you do not cook the fish right away, after 12 hours remove the porgies from the marinade and refrigerate them for up to 12 hours longer before cooking.)

In a shallow bowl or pie plate, combine the flour, cornmeal, salt, and pepper. Remove the fish fillets from the marinade, letting the excess run back into the bowl. Dredge the fillets in the cornmeal mixture to lightly coat both sides; shake off any excess.

Preheat the oven to 350°F.

Pour enough oil into a large skillet (preferably cast iron) to coat the bottom of the pan, and set over medium heat. When the oil is hot, about 350°F, place the fish in the skillet, skin side down. Cook for 2 minutes. Turn the fillets and cook for another 2 minutes. Remove the fillets from the skillet and place on a baking sheet. Bake for 4 to 5 minutes, or until the fish is cooked through yet firm to the touch.

Cornmeal can be blue, white, or yellow, and the texture can vary from fine to coarse. In Southern cooking it is often used as a flour or a coating agent.

Pan-Fried Catfish

Makes 6 servings

For the sherried buttermilk marinade
3 cups buttermilk
½ cup sherry
1 tablespoon sherry vinegar plus 1 tablespoon white wine vinegar
2 tablespoons celery seeds
1½ tablespoons garlic powder
1 tablespoon paprika
1 teaspoon freshly ground black pepper
1 teaspoon salt

Six 8- to 10-ounce catfish fillets (preferably farm-raised)

For the breading
1½ cups all-purpose flour
1 cup fine yellow cornmeal
2 tablespoons garlic powder
1 tablespoon chili powder
1 tablespoon salt
1 tablespoon cayenne pepper
1 tablespoon freshly ground black pepper
1½ cups vegetable oil

Catfish are bottom-dwellers, so they pick up a distinctive earthy flavor. Today most catfish are farmed-raised, which means they are bred in pretty clear water and are fed wheat and corn pellets. This makes the fish a lot sweeter and more subtle in flavor. This fish can be eaten with just a squeeze of lemon or served with Bread-n-Butter Pickle Mayonnaise (page 71).

* * *

In a large bowl, whisk together all the marinade ingredients. Place the catfish in a large shallow dish. Pour the marinade over the fish, cover the dish with plastic wrap, and refrigerate for 24 hours.

In a shallow bowl or pie plate, combine all the breading ingredients. Remove the catfish from the marinade, letting the excess run back into the dish. Dredge the fillets in the breading mixture to lightly coat both sides; shake off any excess.

In a large skillet (preferably cast iron), heat the oil over medium heat. When the oil is hot, about 350°F, carefully lower the fillets into the pan. Cook until the fillets are lightly browned and the flesh is opaque throughout when flaked with a fork, 3 to 5 minutes on each side. Use a slotted spatula to remove the fish to a warmed serving plate.

Bourbon-Cured Salmon

½ cup granulated sugar
¼ cup salt
½ cup chopped fresh cilantro
  leaves
⅓ cup bourbon
¼ cup grated fresh ginger
1 tablespoon sesame seed oil

2 tablespoons fresh lemon juice
1 tablespoon soy sauce
½ teaspoon Chili Paste
  (page 70) or Thai chili paste
2½ pounds boneless salmon
  fillet, skin on

The need to cure and preserve food dates back to early man. Almost every country has dishes that feature preserved foods. Gravlax (*gravad lax*) is a traditional Swedish recipe that employs the art of preserving. Classically, this recipe requires salmon, sugar, salt, dill, and lemon juice. Serve this, thinly sliced, with cucumbers and cream cheese.

* * *

In a small bowl, stir together all the ingredients except the salmon. Using a spoon, spread the curing mixture over the top (skinless) side of the salmon. Wrap the salmon tightly in plastic wrap and place it in a medium-size roasting pan. Weight down the salmon with something heavy, such as cans. Refrigerate for 2 days.

Remove the salmon from the refrigerator and scrape off all the curing mixture. Slice thin, and serve. Wrap any leftovers tightly and refrigerate for up to 10 days.

Buttermilk-Dipped Trout with Stewed Okra

1 cup buttermilk
½ cup all-purpose flour
1 tablespoon garlic powder
1 tablespoon onion salt
1 teaspoon freshly ground black pepper

Four to six 8-ounce trout, boned, heads off
3 tablespoons vegetable oil
Lemon wedges, for serving
1 recipe Stewed Okra (page 102)
1 recipe White Rice (page 82)

Makes 4 to 6 servings

Trout is a freshwater fish. It is pretty common and can be found in the seafood section of most grocery stores. Trout can be prepared by sautéing, frying, or grilling. Be careful—this fish cooks up pretty quickly, and it will dry out and fall apart if it is overcooked.

* * *

Preheat the oven to 350°F.

Pour the buttermilk into a medium bowl. In another bowl mix together the flour, garlic powder, onion salt, and pepper. Submerge the fish completely in the buttermilk. Remove them from the buttermilk, letting the excess run off. Dredge in the flour mixture so the whole fish is coated. Shake off any excess flour mixture.

Heat the oil in a large skillet over medium heat. Place the fish in the pan, folded skin side out. Cook for 1 minute. Turn the fish over and cook for 1 minute more. Remove the fish from the skillet and place them on a baking sheet. Bake for 6 to 10 minutes, or until cooked through. Serve with the lemon wedges, Stewed Okra, and rice.

Pan-Seared Pompano with Southern Summer Ratatouille

Makes 4 to 6 servings

¼ cup vegetable oil
Salt and freshly ground black
  pepper
4 to 6 pompano fillets
½ cup Chicken Stock or
  Vegetable Stock
  (page 6 or 8)

1 recipe Southern Summer
  Ratatouille (page 107)
1 recipe White Rice (page 82)

Pompano is considered by many Americans to be the best fish around. Unfortunately it can get a little pricey. It is a saltwater type of fish, moderately fatty, with a firm texture.

* * *

Preheat the oven to 350°F.

Heat the oil in a heavy-bottom skillet over medium heat. Sprinkle salt and pepper to taste on both sides of the fish fillets. Place the fillets in the pan and cook for 1 minute. Turn them over and cook for 1 minute more. Place the fish on a baking sheet.

Bake for 5 to 7 minutes or until the fish is cooked through. (The time may vary because of the thickness of the fish.) Add the stock to the ratatouille and heat it in a saucepan over medium heat until hot. Remove the fish from the oven and arrange the fillets on plates. Pour the ratatouille over the fish, and serve with the rice.

Braised Red Snapper in Creole Sauce

1 tablespoon Marv Spice
(page 64)
Four to six 6- to 8-ounce red
snapper fillets
¼ cup vegetable oil

2½ cups Creole Sauce
(page 12)
1 recipe Five-Greens Rice
(page 86)

Red Snapper is a popular fish. It can grow up to 35 pounds, although I like to work with the 2- to 3-pounders. The texture of snapper is firm and the meat is white. It is normally found in salt waters from North Carolina to the Gulf of Mexico.

Red snapper can be cooked virtually any way you like. I'm suggesting that you serve this dish with Five-Greens Rice, but you can serve it with white, brown, or wild rice—they will all work just fine.

* * *

Preheat the oven to 350°F.

Sprinkle Marv Spice to taste on both sides of the fish.

Heat the oil in a heavy-bottom skillet over medium heat. Pan-sear the fish on one side for 1½ to 2 minutes. (Rule of thumb: Always sear first the side that you are going to serve.) Turn the fillets over and cook for 1 minute more. Transfer the fish to a roasting pan or glass baking dish. Pour the Creole Sauce over the fish and place in the oven. Bake for 7 to 10 minutes (the time may vary because of the thickness of the fish). Serve with the rice.

Carolina Crab Cakes with Dill Lemon Dressing

Makes 4 to 6 servings

3 tablespoons plus ½ cup vegetable oil
¼ cup finely chopped red bell pepper
¼ cup finely chopped celery
¼ cup finely chopped onion
1 pound fresh Dungeness crabmeat, picked through
¼ cup minced fresh dill (dried will not do)
2 tablespoons Marv Spice (page 64)

2 tablespoons Dijon mustard
1 cup corn flakes, slightly crushed
3 to 5 large egg whites
Dried bread crumbs (preferably Japanese *panko*), for thickening if needed
Dill Lemon Dressing (recipe follows) or lemon wedges, for serving

Crab cakes are an old favorite, but it's hard sometimes to find good ones when we eat out. Well, not to worry—now you are going to have your own recipe, so when you want good crab cakes, you can make them. Let me begin by saying that you must start with good crabmeat to make a good crab cake—which is where plenty of people go wrong. The crabmeat that you want to use for this recipe is called Dungeness, lump, or jumbo lump, and it can be found in the seafood section of most local groceries. ("Pasteurized" crabmeat has been treated to kill all the bacteria, giving it more of a shelf life. It will last up to 5 months unopened in the refrigerator. Once it is opened, you should use it within 4 days.)

＊　＊　＊

Preheat the oven to 350°F.

In a large skillet, heat 3 tablespoons of the oil over medium-high heat. Add the vegetables and cook, stirring, until they become soft (do not let them brown), 2 to 3 minutes. Transfer the vegetables to a large bowl and let cool for a few minutes.

Add the crabmeat, dill, Marv Spice, mustard, and corn flakes to the vegetables. Beat 3 of the egg whites and add them. Work everything together. The mixture should be moist enough to stick together; if it is not, add the remaining 1 or 2 egg whites (beaten). If the mixture seems too loose, add some of the bread crumbs to the mixture. Shape the mixture into balls. Using a large (2- to 3-inch-diameter) cookie cutter, shape the cakes by packing them down and make them flat and round at the same time.

Heat the remaining ½ cup oil in a skillet over medium heat. Place a few crab cakes at a time in the pan and cook until golden brown, 2 to 3 minutes. Turn the crab cakes over and cook another 2 to 3 minutes. Remove from the pan and place on a baking sheet. Cook the remaining crab cakes and transfer them all to the baking sheet.

Place the baking sheet in the oven and bake for 7 to 10 minutes, or until the crab cakes are hot in the middle. Serve with the Dill Lemon Dressing or lemon wedges.

Dill Lemon Dressing

Makes 1 cup

1 tablespoon Dijon mustard
½ cup mayonnaise
¼ cup finely chopped scallions
¼ cup fresh lemon juice

1 tablespoon white wine vinegar
2 tablespoons finely chopped
  fresh dill

You can serve this dressing with most fish dishes or even toss it in a salad.

* * *

Mix all the ingredients in a bowl. Chill until ready to serve. The dressing can be stored up to 7 days, covered, in the refrigerator.

Caramelized Wild Striped Bass

2 tablespoons vegetable oil
Four 8-ounce fillets wild striped
  bass, unskinned

Salt and freshly ground black
  pepper to taste

Makes 4 servings

I like working with striped bass because it has a mild sweet flavor. The meat is firm and white and contains a moderate amount of fat, which keeps it moist in most cooking methods.

Technically, to caramelize means to heat sugar until it becomes a clear syrup, which turns from gold to dark brown according to how long you cook it. Also, when sugar is sprinkled on food and then broiled, it melts or caramelizes. In the case of this recipe, you get a caramelized effect by sautéing wild striped bass skin side down. The fat content in the fish is the secret—and is also the reason why this fish cooks up exceptionally moist (it works with snapper also). This is by far one of my favorite dishes, and it requires only a couple of ingredients (no sugar!). Serve it with Wilted Greens with Herb Vinaigrette (page 52) or Sautéed Collard Greens (page 98).

✳ ✳ ✳

In a large skillet, heat the oil over medium heat. Add the bass to the skillet, skin side down, and cook until the skin forms a crust, 2 to 3 minutes. Turn the fish over to the flesh side and cook for 3 to 4 minutes longer. (Alternatively, you can place the fish in a preheated 350°F oven for the final cooking.) Taste and check the seasoning, adding salt and pepper if needed.

Colombo-Dusted
Sea Scallops

Makes 4 servings

¼ cup cumin seeds
2 tablespoons coriander seeds
1 tablespoon yellow mustard
   seeds
1 tablespoon whole cloves
1 tablespoon crushed red pepper
   flakes
5 tablespoons ground turmeric
2 tablespoons ground cinnamon

2 tablespoons ground ginger
2 tablespoons *garam masala*
   (available in Indian food
   stores)
1½ teaspoons celery salt
½ cup sunflower seeds
12 sea scallops
3 tablespoons vegetable oil

In the French Caribbean islands, *colombo* is the word for curry powder. You can buy ready-made packages of this spice mixture in Guadeloupe. Curry spices came to the Low Country by way of East Indian traders and travelers.

Serve these scallops with rice and a salad.

* * *

In an electric spice grinder, grind the cumin seeds, coriander seeds, mustard seeds, and cloves. Add the red pepper flakes and grind it all to a powder. Remove the mixture from the grinder and place it in a medium bowl. Stir in the turmeric, cinnamon, ginger, garam masala, and celery salt. Add the sunflower seeds to the grinder and process to a powder. Stir the ground sunflower seeds into the mixture in the bowl.

Add the scallops to the bowl and coat them with the mixture on all sides.

In a large skillet, heat the oil over medium heat. Place the scallops in the pan and sauté for 2 minutes (a crust will form). Turn the scallops and sauté again for 2 minutes. If the scallops are very large, you will need to turn them over again and cook for an additional minute on each side (or finish them in a preheated 350°F oven) until they are somewhat firm, 2 to 3 minutes. Remove the scallops from the skillet and serve immediately.

Monkfish and Sweet Sausage Gumbo

¼ cup vegetable oil
2½ pounds monkfish fillet, cut into large dice
1 cup Italian sweet sausage
1 cup ½-inch-thick slices fresh okra
¼ cup finely chopped onion

1 cup canned peeled whole plum tomatoes, chopped, undrained
¼ cup dry white wine
3 cups Creole Sauce (page 12)
2 tablespoons Marv Spice (page 64)

Makes 4 to 6 servings

Monkfish is known as the "poor man's lobster" and can be used instead of lobster in many dishes. It doesn't taste exactly like lobster, but the texture is very close.

Monkfish is also known as angler fish. This fish is low in fat and firm in texture, and it has a mild sweet taste. This is one of my favorite fish because of the texture and the way it cooks up. You can cook monkfish any way you like and it will come out good. Serve this gumbo in a bowl over white rice.

* * *

Heat the oil in a large saucepan over medium heat. Place the diced monkfish in the pan and cook for 2 to 3 minutes. Turn the fish over and add the sausage, okra, onion, and tomato. Cook for 5 minutes, stirring frequently. Add the wine and cook until it has evaporated, 2 to 3 minutes. Add the Creole Sauce and bring to a boil. Reduce the heat and let simmer for 5 to 7 minutes. Add the Marv Spice and taste; add salt and pepper if needed.

Ribs, Chops, and Loins

In the South, the preparation of meats took its cues from all over. The English and French brought with them their knowledge of butchering, curing, pickling, and drying. Africans lent their knowledge of preparing large pieces of tough meat. The first form of barbecuing was to dig a large pit, put the meat inside, and cover it to cook over smoldering embers for 2 to 3 days. Not exactly what we do today, but that was the beginning.

In the Low Country the key to properly barbecued meats is a piquant vinegar marinade. All other types of barbecue were dismissed in Low-Country kitchens as "country cooking."

Barbecued Short Ribs

Makes 4 servings

4 to 5 pounds beef short ribs
½ cup white balsamic vinegar
  or white wine vinegar
3 tablespoons salt
2 tablespoons whole black
  peppercorns

1 bay leaf
2½ cups Burner's Que
  (page 10) or your favorite
  barbecue sauce

These are my favorite ribs for two reasons. First, because of the amount of meat you get to sink your teeth into, as opposed to pork ribs. Some folks might feel that they are too much work because they are cooked for a long period of time over low heat, but the tender and meaty dish you get after that is well worth it. The second reason I love them is because short ribs are an inexpensive cut of meat. I'm telling you, make this recipe and you'll be repeating it for years to come for family and friends.

* * *

Place all the ingredients except the Burner's Que in a large saucepan or soup pot. Heat to a boil over high heat. Reduce the heat and let simmer for 45 minutes, or until the meat starts to pull away from the bone.

Remove the ribs from the pot and roll them in the Burner's Que while they are still hot. They are ready to eat now, but for that extra-special touch, place the ribs on a medium hot grill (or under the broiler) and let them pick up a little smoky flavor. Brush them with a little extra sauce before serving.

Spare Ribs

3 racks pork ribs, 12 ribs each
1 onion
1 bay leaf
¼ cup whole black peppercorns
¼ cup white wine vinegar

Salt to taste
1½ cups Burner's Que
(page 10) or your favorite
barbecue sauce

Makes 4 to 6 servings

Spare ribs come from the pig's breastbone. They don't really contain a lot of meat, but they are fattier than beef ribs, which makes them quite juicy. Spare ribs, another staple of the South, are prepared in many different ways, from smoking to barbecuing. Like most inexpensive cuts of meat, if not cooked properly, they can become tough and sometimes dry.

*　*　*

Place all the ingredients except the Burner's Que in a large soup pot. Heat to a boil. Reduce the heat and let simmer for 45 minutes, or until the meat starts to pull away from the bone.

Remove the ribs from the pot and roll them in the Burner's Que while they are still hot. They are ready to eat now, but for that extra-special touch, place the ribs on a medium-hot grill (or in a roasting pan in a preheated 350°F oven) and let the sauce cook onto the ribs.

Roast Pork Tenderloin with Brown Sugar Pineapple Jam

Makes 6 to 8 servings

2½ pounds tenderloin of pork
½ cup orange juice
¼ cup bourbon
2 tablespoons Marv Spice
(page 64)

2 tablespoons vegetable oil
1½ cups Brown Sugar Pineapple
Jam (recipe follows)

Pork is one of those ingredients that have always been associated with the South. It was inexpensive and in abundance in Early American times, so it was a large part of the slave diet. For this particular recipe we use the tenderloin, which is a pretty lean piece of meat. In the past 7 to 10 years the production of pork has changed so much that we can now enjoy it at a medium doneness. That means it needs to reach an internal temperature of 150°F. You must still follow the normal precautions when handling pork, like washing your cutting board, hands, and knife in hot soapy water. Keep in mind that cooking the pork longer than needed doesn't make it any safer and makes the flavor a lot less desirable. Do not let the meat stand for longer than 2 hours at room temperature.

* * *

Place the meat in a bowl or roasting pan. Add the orange juice and bourbon. Roll the meat in the liquid. Sprinkle the Marv Spice evenly over the meat. Let the meat rest for 20 to 30 minutes. This will allow for the marinade to soak in and for the meat to come to room temperature. (Tip: It is always better to prepare meat from room temperature than refrigerator-cold.)

Meanwhile, preheat the oven to 450°F.

Place the oil in a heavy-bottom skillet over medium-high heat. Sear the meat on all sides for 1½ to 2 minutes. Transfer the meat to a roasting pan and roast it in the oven for about 8 minutes. Turn the pork over and roast for another 8 minutes or until it reaches an internal temperature of 150°F. Remove the pan from the oven and transfer the pork to a plate to rest for 5 minutes (this will allow the meat to stop cooking and the juices to settle). While the pork is resting, heat the Brown Sugar Pineapple Jam in a medium saucepan over low heat until warm. Slice the pork and arrange it on a plate. Drizzle the jam over the pork and serve.

Brown Sugar Pineapple Jam

Makes about 2½ cups

1 tablespoon vegetable oil
½ onion, finely chopped
2 tablespoons minced fresh
 ginger
One 2-pound pineapple, peeled,
 cored, and finely chopped
1½ cups firmly packed brown
 sugar

¾ cup raspberry vinegar
½ cup granulated sugar
¼ cup finely chopped cilantro
 leaves
¼ cup dried tart cherries
1 teaspoon salt
½ teaspoon lemon juice

Brown sugar is white sugar that has some molasses added to it. Light brown sugar has a more delicate molasses flavor, while the flavor of dark brown sugar is more robust. The sweet and sour flavor of this jam pairs well with most spicy meat dishes. It gives a nice balance to the meal.

* * *

In a large saucepan, heat the oil over medium heat. Add the onion and ginger and cook, stirring, until the onions become transparent, about 2 minutes. Stir in all the remaining ingredients. Reduce the heat to low and let simmer, stirring occasionally, until most of the liquid has evaporated, about 1½ hours. Cover and refrigerate; this will keep for up to 4 weeks.

Chicken-Fried Steak

1 teaspoon salt
1 teaspoon freshly ground black
  pepper
Six 6-ounce filet mignon steaks,
  pounded to ¼-inch thickness
¼ cup Dijon mustard
2 tablespoons fresh rosemary
  leaves, or 1 tablespoon dried,
  chopped

2 cups dry bread crumbs
  (preferably Japanese *panko*)
1 cup all-purpose flour
4 large egg whites, lightly beaten
½ cup vegetable, corn, or
  olive oil

Makes 6 servings

Panko bread crumbs have long been used in Japanese kitchens as a coating for fried foods. Today you will find most good chefs use them because they give the food a lighter and crunchier texture than any other type of bread crumb. You can find them in Asian markets and most gourmet stores.

Chicken-fried steak is not only big in the South, it is a favorite in the Midwest as well. Initially, this technique was created to make use of inexpensive cuts of meat. The meat was tenderized by being pounded into thin steaks, then dipped into an egg/milk mixture and seasoned flour. It was then fried like chicken until crispy and brown. I recommend using a good cut of meat, like filet mignon if you can afford it, and then cooking it until medium-rare. Serve it as it is, or with Pan Gravy (page 18), Gingersnap Gravy (page 17), or any barbecue sauce. Any way you dish it up, it is sure to be good.

* * *

Evenly sprinkle the salt and pepper on both sides of the filets. In a small bowl, stir together the mustard and rosemary. Using a brush, coat each side of the steaks with the mustard mixture. In a shallow bowl or pie plate, combine the bread crumbs and flour. Dip the steaks in the egg whites and then dip them into the bread crumb mixture.

In a large skillet (preferably cast iron), heat the oil over medium heat. Place a steak in the pan. For medium-rare, cook the steak for 1 minute, turn, and cook the other side for 1 more minute. If you would like your steak to be more done, increase the cooking time.

Bourbon-Soaked Pork Chops

Makes 4 servings

For the bourbon marinade
1 cup bourbon
¾ cup orange juice
¼ cup fresh lemon juice
2 tablespoons vegetable oil
1 tablespoon vanilla extract
1 teaspoon ground
  cinnamon
1 teaspoon ground nutmeg

1 teaspoon Chili Paste
  (page 70) or crushed red
  pepper flakes
1 teaspoon salt

Four 8-ounce center-cut pork
  chops
Brown Sugar Honey Glaze
  (recipe follows)

Bourbon is really the only distinct American spirit. Its name comes from Bourbon County, Virginia, and it arrived on the scene around 1789. Now most bourbon is produced in Kentucky. Besides consuming it straight from the bottle as a beverage, we use bourbon in everything from appetizers to desserts. Serve these chops with Brown Sugar Honey Glaze and Wild Rice (page 88).

* * *

In a medium bowl, stir together all of the marinade ingredients. Place the pork chops in a deep baking dish that is large enough to hold them in a single layer. Pour the marinade mixture over the pork chops, cover, and refrigerate for at least 24 hours and up to 36 hours, turning occasionally.

Position a grill or broiler 5 to 6 inches away from the heat source. Remove the chops from the marinade and grill or broil for about 10 minutes on each side, or until cooked through. Brush the Brown Sugar Honey Glaze on both sides of the chops in the final cooking process, about 2 minutes.

Brown Sugar Honey Glaze

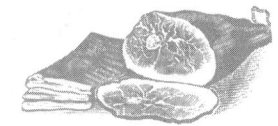

¾ cup honey
¼ cup firmly packed dark brown
  sugar
⅛ cup hoisin sauce
⅛ cup fresh lemon juice

1 tablespoon soy sauce
½ tablespoon grated fresh ginger
1 teaspoon minced garlic
1 teaspoon Marv Spice
  (page 64)

Makes about 1¼ cups

This flavorful sauce with an Asian accent can be used in place of most barbecue sauces. I especially like it on spare ribs, pork, and lamb.

* * *

In a medium saucepan, combine the honey and brown sugar and cook over low heat, stirring frequently, until the sugar is dissolved. Stir in all the remaining ingredients. Simmer for 5 minutes, stirring occasionally. Cover and refrigerate for up to 1 month.

Spicy Pulled Pork Shoulder

Makes 8 to 10 servings

2 cloves garlic, minced

2 tablespoons chopped fresh rosemary leaves, or 1 tablespoon dried

2 tablespoons chopped fresh sage leaves, or 1 tablespoon dried

2 tablespoons chopped fresh thyme leaves, or 1 tablespoon dried

1 tablespoon Chili Paste (page 70), or 1 tablespoon Tabasco sauce plus 1 tablespoon Worcestershire sauce

1 tablespoon salt

1 tablespoon cayenne pepper

1 tablespoon freshly ground black pepper

One 6- to 8-pound boneless pork shoulder

½ celery rib, coarsely chopped

2 onions, coarsely chopped

3 carrots, coarsely chopped

2 cups water

Put this on a nice onion brioche with some Burner's Que (page 10), serve it with a starch and a vegetable, and go to town.

*   *   *

Preheat the oven to 350°F.

In a small bowl, stir together the garlic, herbs, Chili Paste, salt, and both peppers. Rub the pork all over with the mixture. Tie the pork before cooking (see Note).

Place the vegetables in the bottom of a roasting pan, and cover with the water. Place the pork on top of the vegetables and cook for 40 minutes. Turn the pork. Continue cooking for about 40 minutes per pound, or until the pork is tender enough to be shredded with a fork.

When the pork is done, remove it from the pan. Let the meat cool down to the point where you can work with it without burning yourself. Using a fork, pull pieces off until you have shredded all the meat. (There may be some big pieces that you have to cut with a knife.)

Transfer the vegetables and juices in the bottom of the pan to a blender or a food processor fitted with the metal chopping blade. Process until almost smooth. Strain through a medium sieve. Serve this as a sauce, a spread, or add chicken or vegetable stock and use to reheat the pork in.

Note: Ask the butcher to bone the shoulder. Basically, you want to tie the pork several (five to seven) rings around to ensure that it doesn't fall apart during the cooking process. Leave 1 to 2 inches between the rings.

Pork Chops Smothered with Peppers and Onions

Makes 4 servings

2 large egg whites
Four 7- to 8-ounce center-cut
  pork chops
2 tablespoons chopped fresh
  rosemary leaves, or 1
  tablespoon dried
1½ teaspoons garlic powder
1 teaspoon salt
1 teaspoon freshly ground
  black pepper
¼ cup all-purpose flour

¼ cup vegetable oil
2 red bell peppers, cut into
  julienne strips
1 green bell pepper, cut into
  julienne strips
1 onion, cut into julienne strips
½ cup Chicken Stock or Veal or
  Beef Stock (page 6 or 7)
2 to 4 tablespoons all-purpose
  flour (optional)

In the pre–Civil War South, a slave's diet was determined by the slave owner's attitude. Pork and corn were basic weekly food rations throughout the South. But on the Low-Country plantations life was usually different because of the natural food resources of the land. Most slaves received various foods, including sweet potatoes, peas, turnips, seasonal fruits, beef, mutton, salted fish, coffee, molasses, and, on rice plantations, rice. Other slaves were given their own plot of land on which to raise vegetables as well as hogs and chickens. Some slave owners, especially in the Low Country, allowed their slaves to go hunting and keep whatever they caught.

To this day, pork is still a very big part of the Southerner's diet.

* * *

Place the egg whites in a shallow dish and lightly beat together. Dip each pork chop in the whites until it is completely covered, and set aside. In a small bowl, stir together the rosemary, garlic powder, salt, and pepper. Sprinkle the mixture over both sides of the pork chops, and then dust the pork chops lightly with the flour.

In a large skillet, heat the oil over medium heat. When the oil is hot (check by dipping a tip of the pork chop in the oil or by checking a fry thermometer), add the pork chops. Cook the chops until golden brown, 4 to 5 minutes. Turn and cook the other side for 4 to 5 minutes. Using a slotted spatula, remove the pork chops from the pan and reserve.

Add the bell peppers and onion to the same skillet and cook, stirring, until the vegetables start to soften, 3 to 4 minutes. Add the stock and bring the mixture to a simmer. Return the pork chops to the skillet and cover. Cook over low heat until the pork chops are cooked through, 10 to 15 minutes. When the chops are cooked, check the consistency of the sauce. If you would like it to be thicker, remove the chops and sift in a little flour. Let the mixture simmer until it thickens.

Roast Tenderloin of Beef with Rosemary and Roasted Shallot Pan Gravy

Makes 6 servings

2½ pounds tenderloin of beef
1 tablespoon Worcestershire
  sauce
3 tablespoons olive oil

3 tablespoons Marv's Garlic Rub
  (page 76)
1½ cups Roasted Shallot Pan
  Gravy (recipe follows)

This tenderloin is also known as fillet strip and fillet of beef, and when it is cut into steaks they are called filet mignon. This particular cut of meat is very lean and tender. When meat is lean like this, it doesn't have a lot of fat running through, as you see with some other cuts. What this means is that if you cook it to well-done, it can become tough. So I recommend not to cook it past medium doneness.

* * *

Preheat the oven to 450°F.

Cut the tenderloin across into 2 pieces. Place them in a large bowl and pour in the Worcestershire sauce and 1 tablespoon of the oil. Roll the meat in the liquid. Then pour off the liquid and sprinkle the Garlic Rub all over the meat.

Heat the remaining 2 tablespoons oil in a heavy-bottom skillet over medium heat. Place the meat in the pan and sear for 1½ to 2 minutes on all sides. Remove from the pan, place in a roasting pan, and transfer to the oven.

Roast the tenderloin for 15 to 20 minutes, turning the meat over at the halfway point. Test after 15 minutes of cooking for medium-rare. Using a meat thermometer, the internal temperature should read 120° to 125°F. If you must eat it well-done, leave it in the oven for another 7 to 10 minutes. Be sure to check the doneness with your thermometer because the cooking time can vary depending on the thickness of the meat. Remove the meat from the oven, place it on a cutting board, and let it rest for about 5 minutes. (This allows the meat to stop cooking and the juices to settle.) While the meat is resting, heat the Roasted Shallot Pan Gravy in a medium saucepan over medium heat. Slice the meat to the desired thickness, drizzle the gravy over the top, and serve.

Rosemary has silvery green needle-like leaves and is highly aromatic. You can find fresh rosemary year-round at your local supermarket.

Roasted Shallot Pan Gravy

Makes 1¾ cups

1 tablespoon vegetable oil
½ cup sliced Roasted Shallots
  (page 74)
2 tablespoons finely chopped
  fresh rosemary, or 1 tablespoon
  crumbled dried rosemary

1 tablespoon all-purpose flour
1½ cups Veal or Beef Stock
  (page 7)
Salt and freshly ground black
  pepper to taste

* * *

Heat the oil in a small saucepan over medium heat. Add the shallots and cook, stirring, for 1½ to 2 minutes. Add the rosemary and flour. Turn the heat to low. Stir and cook for another minute. Add the stock slowly, stirring constantly with a wire whisk until all the liquid is added. Simmer for 10 to 12 minutes, until you can't taste the flour anymore. Add salt and pepper to taste.

Grilled Filet Mignon with Brown Oyster Gravy

1 pound filet mignon
¼ cup Garlic Oil (page 73) or other garlic-infused oil
1 tablespoon minced Roasted Garlic (page 73) or raw garlic
1 tablespoon Chili Paste (page 70) or Chili Rub (page 75), or use a store-bought brand
2 teaspoons finely chopped fresh thyme leaves, or 1 teaspoon dried
2 teaspoons finely chopped fresh rosemary leaves, or 1 teaspoon dried

2 teaspoons finely chopped fresh sage leaves, or 1 teaspoon dried
Salt and freshly ground black pepper to taste
6 oysters, shucked, liquor reserved
¼ cup fine yellow cornmeal
2 tablespoons vegetable oil
1 cup clam juice
1 cup Demi-Glace Sauce (page 16)
2 tablespoons unsalted butter (optional)

Makes 4 to 6 servings

Oysters are in abundance and are frequently used in Low-Country cooking. Here is my take on "Surf and Turf." I chose filet mignon because of its tender buttery texture. While tender, however, it is not the most flavorful cut of beef. The oysters add the flavor. Feel free to substitute another steak, such as sirloin or ribeye.

If you don't have demi-glace, use canned beef and mushroom soup and strain out the mushrooms.

* * *

Place the filet mignon in a glass dish and rub with the Garlic Oil, garlic, Chili Paste, 1 teaspoon each of the thyme, rosemary, and sage, and salt and pepper to taste. Let stand for 30 minutes.

Dredge the oysters in the cornmeal to lightly coat, shaking off any excess. Heat the vegetable oil in a large skillet over medium heat. Add the oysters and cook for 1 minute. Using a slotted spoon, transfer the oysters to a plate. Gradually whisk the clam juice and reserved oyster liquor into the skillet and continue cooking until the sauce is reduced by half, 5 to 7 minutes. Add the Demi-Glace and remaining 1 teaspoon of each of the herbs, and simmer over low heat until the sauce thickens, 7 to 10 minutes. Use the crisp oysters as a garnish, and add the butter, if using. Taste and check the seasoning, adding salt if needed. Turn the heat down and keep the mixture warm until the filet is done.

Place a grill rack 5 to 6 inches above medium-hot coals. Season the filet mignon with salt and pepper on both sides, and place it on the rack. Grill for 7 minutes, then turn over to cook for another 7 minutes. Check with a meat thermometer if you like; the meat will be rare. If you like it more done, cook it for 2 to 3 more minutes on each side (be sure to cook it equally on both sides). Serve the filet with the sauce.

Braised Oxtail

Makes 4 servings

6 pounds oxtails
1 teaspoon salt
4 teaspoons freshly ground black pepper
1½ cups all-purpose flour
½ cup vegetable oil
3 carrots, finely chopped
1½ onions, finely chopped
½ celery rib, finely chopped
2 cloves garlic, minced
1 tablespoon tomato paste
2 cups inexpensive red wine, such as a Burgundy or Cabernet
¼ cup balsamic vinegar
1½ quarts Chicken Stock or Beef or Veal Stock (page 6 or 7)
10 to 12 sprigs fresh thyme, tied together, or 2 tablespoons dried
4 russet potatoes, cut into 1-inch cubes
Salt to taste

Much of West African cooking is based on one-pot dishes, so this recipe, inspired by this unique cuisine, fits right in with the cooking of the Low Country as well as many other Southern regions. Using this cut of the meat is another example of making the whole animal productive. An inexpensive cut, oxtail has lots of flavor. Much of the meat is encased in the bone, which is why it has a lengthy cooking time. Normally oxtail is sold cut into pieces. If it isn't, ask the butcher to cut them into 4- to 8-ounce pieces. You may omit the potatoes and serve this with white rice, mashed potatoes, or baked potatoes.

* * *

Sprinkle the oxtail with 1 teaspoon of the salt and 2 teaspoons of the pepper. Dredge the oxtail in 1 cup of the flour to lightly coat. Shake off any excess.

In a large saucepan or soup pot, heat the oil over medium-high heat. Place the oxtail in the pan and sear for 2 to 3 minutes per side until the oxtail is lightly browned on all sides. Remove the oxtail from the pan. Add the carrots, onion, and celery to the same pan and reduce the heat to low. Cook, stirring, until the vegetables begin to soften, 5 to 7 minutes. Add the garlic and cook, stirring, for 2 minutes longer. Stir in the remaining ½ cup flour and the tomato paste. Add the red wine and balsamic vinegar and simmer until almost all the liquid is gone, 5 to 7 minutes. Add the stock, reserved oxtail, thyme, and remaining 2 teaspoons pepper. Cover and cook for 1 hour over low heat, stirring occasionally. Skim any fat from the surface. Add the potatoes. Taste, adding salt if needed. Cook 30 minutes longer, or until the potatoes are just tender. Remove the thyme sprigs if using fresh and serve.

Yard Birds

I n the early 1700s, the forests and wetlands of the Low Country were filled with quail, snipes, pheasant, woodcocks, duck, partridge, and turkey. The birds at their doorsteps, combined with the availability of exotic spices in port cities like Charleston and Savannah, created signature poultry dishes.

No cookbook about Southern cooking would be complete without a fried chicken recipe. To make a good thing better, my Low-Country style is to marinate the poultry in buttermilk, which contains enough acid to tenderize but not enough to pulverize the texture. Spend a little extra on a free-range bird. I guarantee, it does make a difference in the taste.

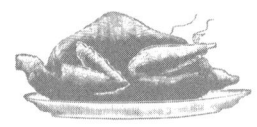

Southern-Exposed Fried Chicken

For the buttermilk marinade
1 quart buttermilk
1 tablespoon paprika
1 tablespoon garlic powder
1¼ teaspoons salt
1¼ teaspoons freshly ground
 black pepper
1¼ teaspoons cayenne pepper

One 2- to 3-pound broiler-fryer
 chicken, cut into 6 to 8 pieces

For the breading
3 cups all-purpose flour
2 tablespoons paprika
2 tablespoons freshly ground
 black pepper
1 tablespoon garlic powder
1 tablespoon onion powder
1 tablespoon cayenne pepper
1 tablespoon celery salt
1 tablespoon salt
1½ cups vegetable oil, for frying

Almost everybody likes good fried chicken, but I don't think everybody knows how to *make* good fried chicken. It is best to start with the tastiest meat you can buy, but sometimes mass-produced chicken, even top-quality birds, can use a little extra help. I often use marinades and rubs to give my meat and poultry more character.

In this particular recipe, the most important ingredient is the buttermilk in the marinade. In earlier times, people hand-churned their own butter, so this was a great way to use the liquid that was left over. The acid content of buttermilk lends a tenderizing effect when marinating poultry, fish, or meat.

＊　＊　＊

In a large bowl, stir together all of the marinade ingredients. Place the chicken pieces in a large dish. Pour the marinade over the chicken, cover, and refrigerate for at least 4 hours and up to 24 hours.

Preheat the oven to 350°F.

In a shallow bowl or pie plate, combine all the breading ingredients. Remove the chicken from the marinade, letting the excess run back into the dish. Dredge the chicken in the breading mixture to lightly coat; shake off any excess.

In a large skillet (preferably cast iron), heat the oil over medium heat. When the oil is hot (about 350°F), carefully lower as many pieces of chicken into the pan as will fit without touching. (The chicken needs a little room so it can cook properly.) Cook until the chicken is golden brown, 3 to 5 minutes per side. Using a slotted spoon, transfer the chicken to a baking sheet and bake for 20 to 30 minutes longer, or until cooked through. Check the chicken for doneness by sticking the tip of a knife to the bone to see if the chicken is no longer pink. (If you prefer to finish frying the chicken in the skillet, reduce the heat if necessary so the grease does not get too hot and burn the chicken. Cook the chicken, turning occasionally, until cooked through, about 20 minutes. But do keep in mind that finishing your chicken in the oil makes for a greasier product.)

I don't believe you will have a hard time finding buttermilk, but if you do, you can substitute 1 quart of plain yogurt. Or try a mixture of 1 tablespoon vinegar or lemon juice plus enough milk to equal 1 quart, and let stand for 5 minutes at room temperature.

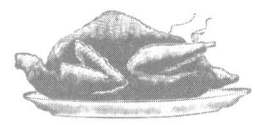

Stewed Chicken

Makes 4 servings

6 chicken legs (thighs and
    drumstick)
1 tablespoon Marv Spice
    (page 64)
½ teaspoon salt
¼ cup vegetable oil
½ cup minced onion
¼ cup minced garlic
½ cup finely diced celery

½ cup finely diced carrots
¼ cup dry white wine
¼ cup all-purpose flour
1¼ cups Chicken Stock
    (page 6)
1 tablespoon fresh thyme leaves,
    or ½ tablespoon dried
1 tablespoon fresh rosemary
    leaves, or ½ tablespoon dried

Stewing is defined as cooking an ingredient (usually a tough piece of meat) by barely covering it with a liquid and simmering it slowly for a long period of time in a tightly covered pot. This method aids in tenderizing meats, which is why I am doing this chicken this way. It is also a way to ensure that you will have good flavor in your end product.

You can add potatoes to this recipe if you wish. Add them just before you are going to put the chicken in the oven for the first time. This dish is also good with most rice dishes.

* * *

Preheat the oven to 200°F.

In a bowl, toss the chicken quarters with the Marv Spice and salt. Add the oil to a Dutch oven or large ovenproof saucepan and heat it over medium heat. Add the chicken and brown on one side for 2 to 3 minutes. Turn the chicken over and brown the other side for 2 to 3 minutes. Remove the chicken from the pan and place in a bowl.

Add the vegetables to the same pan and cook over medium heat, stirring occasionally, until softened, 3 to 5 minutes. Add the white wine and cook, scraping up the bits from the bottom of the pan, for about 1 minute. Add the flour slowly, constantly stirring to prevent any lumps. Put the chicken back in the pan, along with any juices that may have accumulated in the bottom of the bowl. Add the chicken stock and bring to a boil. Reduce the heat to a simmer.

Place a lid or a large sheet of aluminum foil over the top of the pan, transfer it to the oven, and cook for 30 minutes. Add the herbs to the pan, replace the cover, and cook for another 15 minutes or until the internal temperature reaches 165° to 170°F (use a meat thermometer). Taste, add more seasoning if needed, and serve.

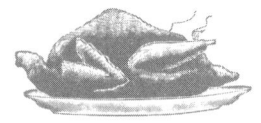

Roasted Chicken

Makes 6 servings

½ teaspoon salt
½ teaspoon freshly ground black
  pepper
1 tablespoon paprika
½ teaspoon celery salt
1 tablespoon vegetable oil

One 3-pound fryer chicken
2 sprigs fresh thyme, or
  3 tablespoons dried
2 sprigs fresh rosemary, or
  3 tablespoons dried
2 cloves garlic

Roasted Chicken is simple to make and is one of my favorite multipurpose recipes. For basics, I'll pair it up, with or without a sauce, with vegetables and a starch. Then I'll let the leftovers cool, slice up the chicken, and make sandwiches with it. I'll even dice the leftovers to make chicken salad.

*   *   *

Preheat the oven to 375°F.

Mix the salt, pepper, paprika, and celery salt together. Rub the oil all over the chicken, and then sprinkle the spice mixture over the chicken. Rub the mixture in a little. Take a sprig of rosemary, a sprig of thyme, and a clove of garlic, and insert them between the skin and the meat on one side of the breast. Repeat this procedure on the other side.

Place a rack in the bottom of a roasting pan. Set the chicken on its side on the rack, and place in the oven. Bake for 20 minutes. Then turn chicken to its other side and bake for 20 minutes more. Turn it breast side up, and roast another 10 minutes. Then check the breast meat with an instant-read thermometer. Once the breast reaches 155°F, measure the thigh temperature, which must be at least 165° to 170°F. When the chicken is done, remove it from the oven and let it sit for 15 to 20 minutes on a cutting board before carving. This resting period will make it easier to carve the chicken.

Burner's Barbecue Chicken

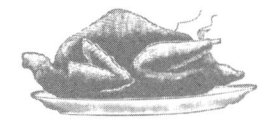

4 pounds chicken parts (thighs, legs, breast, and wings)

2 cups Burner's Que (page 10)

Makes 6 servings

You can use any of the barbecue sauces in this book or your favorite store-brought brand here. This is a recipe that you can make any time of the year because you don't need a grill to cook the chicken. The trick is in marinating the chicken in the barbecue sauce for at least 2 hours so the flavor can soak into the meat.

* * *

Place the chicken in a large bowl. Cover it with the barbecue sauce and refrigerate for at least 2 hours and up to 24 hours.

Preheat the oven to 350°F.

Place the chicken and the sauce in a roasting pan or casserole dish large enough for the pieces not to touch. Bake, uncovered, for 1¼ hours, basting and turning the chicken every 20 minutes. For a true Southern-style dish, serve with macaroni and cheese.

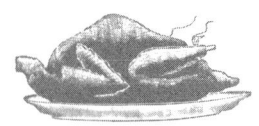

Gingersnap-Braised Chicken

Makes 6 servings

½ cup plain yogurt
One 1-inch piece fresh ginger, minced or grated
1 tablespoon fresh lemon juice
1 teaspoon Marv Spice (page 64)

1 cup Gingersnap Gravy (page 17), plus 1 extra cup if preparing in the oven instead of the grill
4 pounds chicken parts (thighs, legs, breast, wings)

This dish is fairly simple to make and it is a crowd-pleaser. For me, the trick for having good flavor in your dish, especially with meat, is to marinate it. This way you don't necessarily need a sauce and you still have the dancing-on-your-tongue flavor. Make sure the gravy is chilled before using it as a marinade. What sets this dish off is the acid from the yogurt, which will not only add flavor but will also tenderize your chicken. The flavor of the fresh ginger gives this a balance of pepper/sweet taste.

This dish goes well with plain couscous or white, wild, or brown rice.

* * *

Pour the yogurt into a large bowl. Add the ginger, lemon juice, Marv Spice, and 1 cup gravy. Whisk together with a wire whisk until all the ingredients are incorporated. Add the chicken and make sure all the pieces are coated with the marinade. Place in the refrigerator and let marinate for at least 12 hours and up to 36 hours.

If you are using a grill: Light your grill to create a low—medium fire. Shake the excess marinade off the chicken. Cook the chicken on the grill, slowly, for 1 hour. Use a meat thermometer to check that the internal temperature is 170°F. The chicken breast pieces may take only 40 minutes, depending on how big they are.

If you are using the oven: Preheat the oven to 350°F. Shake off the excess marinade and place the chicken in a large roasting pan or casserole dish. Add the extra cup of Gingersnap Gravy to the chicken. Place in the oven and bake for 1¼ hours.

Creole Braised Chicken with Golden Rice

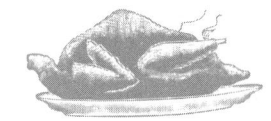

6 chicken legs (thighs and
drumsticks)
Salt and freshly ground black
pepper
½ cup all-purpose flour
2 tablespoons blended oil, or
vegetable or corn oil

1 tablespoon minced fresh garlic
¼ cup minced onion
¼ cup Chicken Stock (page 6)
4 cups Creole Sauce (page 12)
1 recipe Golden Rice (page 92)

Makes 6 servings

Once you make the Creole Sauce, this dish is quick and easy. I pair it with Golden Rice here, but you can replace the rice with anything from mashed potatoes to couscous.

* * *

Place the chicken in a large bowl. Sprinkle it with salt and pepper. Lightly coat the chicken with the flour, shaking off any excess.

Place a large saucepan over medium heat and add the oil. Add the chicken, skin side down, and sear until golden brown, 3 to 5 minutes. Add the garlic and onion and cook, stirring constantly, until softened but not colored, 2 to 3 minutes. Add the stock and Creole Sauce and bring to a boil. Lower the heat and simmer until the chicken pulls away from the bone fairly easily, 45 minutes to 1 hour. Place the rice in a large bowl. Add the chicken and a good amount of the pan juices, and serve.

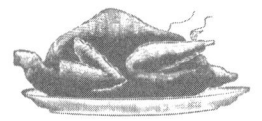

Country Captain Chicken

Makes 4 to 6 servings

1 cup plain yogurt
½ cup tomato paste
3 tablespoons chopped fresh
  mint leaves
2 tablespoons minced garlic
2 tablespoons fresh lemon juice
1 teaspoon curry powder
1 teaspoon chili powder
1 teaspoon ground turmeric
1 teaspoon ground cumin

1 teaspoon ground coriander
1 teaspoon salt
½ teaspoon freshly ground black
  pepper
One 4½- to 5-pound chicken,
  cut into pieces, rinsed and
  patted dry
¼ cup vegetable oil (for oven-
  fry method only)

This dish, my updated version, exemplifies the influence of eastern India on the cuisine of the South. Like many Indian dishes, this chicken dish utilizes yogurt, curry, and mint in the marinade before it is grilled. (I also give directions on how to oven-fry the chicken.) As to how its name came about, there seem to be several theories. One is that it originated with an Indian officer who introduced a sea captain to this dish, who then brought the recipe to the United States.

* * *

In a large bowl, stir together all of the ingredients except the chicken and the oil. Add the chicken and toss to lightly coat with the marinade. Cover with plastic wrap and refrigerate for at least 12 hours and up to 48 hours.

To grill or broil: Remove the chicken from the marinade, letting the excess run back into the bowl. Grill or broil the chicken for 12 to 15 minutes per side, turning occasionally, until it is cooked through and the juices run clear when pierced with the tip of a sharp knife.

To oven-fry: Preheat the oven to 350°F. Heat the vegetable oil in a large skillet. Remove the chicken from the marinade, letting the excess run back into the bowl. Add the chicken to the skillet skin side down, one piece at a time. Cook for 5 to 7 minutes. Turn the chicken and brown the second side for 5 minutes. Transfer the chicken to a baking sheet and bake for 12 to 15 minutes, or until it is cooked through and the juices run clear when pierced with the tip of a sharp knife.

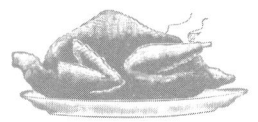

Home-Style Smothered Chicken

Makes 6 to 8 servings

½ cup vegetable oil
Three 2- to 3-pound chickens,
  boned and quartered
Salt and freshly ground black
  pepper to taste
1 onion, sliced
2 tablespoons chopped fresh
  thyme leaves, or 1 tablespoon
  dried

1 cup all-purpose flour
4 cups Chicken Stock (page 6)
2 tablespoons Dijon-style
  mustard

Here's a recipe I attribute to my mom. It's a simple dish that used to frequent our dinner table often. This version has a few more ingredients than the original—me being the chef and all, it's hard for me to be just basic. You'll be happy to know that the added ingredients don't increase the preparation time.

* * *

In a large ovenproof skillet, heat the oil over medium heat. Season the chicken pieces with salt and pepper to taste. Place them in the skillet and cook until browned on all sides, about 2 minutes per side. Using a slotted spoon, transfer the chicken pieces to several layers of paper towels to drain.

Preheat the oven to 350°F.

Add the onion and thyme to the same skillet and cook, stirring, until the onion becomes translucent, about 5 minutes. Whisk in the flour, reduce the heat to low, and cook, stirring constantly, for 5 minutes. Whisk in the chicken stock. Return the chicken pieces to the pan and place in the oven. Bake for 40 minutes, or until the chicken is cooked through. Stir in the mustard. Taste and check the seasoning, adding salt and pepper if needed.

Roasted Farm-Raised Guinea Hen

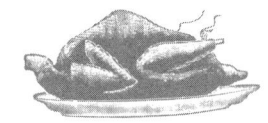

One 2- to 3-pound guinea hen
1 tablespoon vegetable oil
2 cloves garlic, cut in half
4 sprigs fresh thyme, or 1 tablespoon dried

2 teaspoons paprika
1 teaspoon salt
1 teaspoon freshly ground black pepper

Makes 4 servings

Guinea hen falls into the category of game fowl. It tastes like a cross between chicken and pheasant. As with chicken, it must be cooked all the way through, though it does not take as long to cook as chicken. Although most people would cook this versatile bird for dinner, I love roasting guinea hen just to slice up for sandwiches with a bit of Dijon mustard. You can substitute chicken in this recipe.

❋   ❋   ❋

Preheat the oven to 350°F.

Rub the top half of the hen with the oil. Using the tip of a sharp knife, poke a small slit into both sides of the bird, into the skin where the thighs and the breast meet. Place a piece of garlic inside each slit. Place the remaining 2 pieces of garlic and the thyme inside the cavity of the bird. Sprinkle the bird with the paprika, salt, and pepper.

Place the hen in a roasting pan or an ovenproof baking dish. Roast for 30 minutes per pound, or until the juices run clear when the meat is tested with the point of a sharp knife.

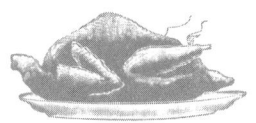

Honey-Orange-Glazed Grilled Muscovy Duck Breast

For the orange glaze
One 6-ounce can frozen orange
  juice concentrate, thawed
¼ cup honey
¼ cup Dijon-style mustard
¼ cup whole-grain mustard
2 tablespoons fresh lemon juice
¼ teaspoon cayenne pepper
¼ teaspoon chili powder
¼ teaspoon freshly grated
  nutmeg
¼ teaspoon freshly ground black
  pepper
Pinch of salt

For the duck
4 to 6 boneless Muscovy duck
  breasts
¼ teaspoon salt
¼ teaspoon freshly ground black
  pepper

Muscovy is a basic type of duck. I like the farm-raised variety because the flavor is toned down and usually appeals to a wider audience. Serve this with Parsnip Mash (page 113) and Sautéed Collard Greens (page 98) or, for a lighter meal, a salad and Sweet Potato Fries (page 110).

* * *

In a medium bowl, stir together all of the glaze ingredients until blended.

Sprinkle the duck breasts with the salt and pepper. Pour half of the glaze mixture into a bowl. Add the duck breast, marinate for 2 hours, cover, and refrigerate.

Prepare a fire for grilling by piling charcoal or lava rocks on each side of the grill, leaving the center empty. Place a drip pan between the coals. Coat the rack with vegetable cooking spray and place on the grill. Remove the breasts from the marinade and shake off the extra. Arrange the breasts, skin side up, over the drip pan. Cover and grill, basting occasionally with the remaining glaze, over medium-high heat (300° to 350°F) for about 25 minutes, or until a meat thermometer inserted into the thickest portion registers 160°F.

Turn the breasts and grill over direct heat for 5 minutes, or until crisp, basting occasionally with the remaining glaze. Transfer the duck to a plate and let the meat rest for 5 minutes. Then slice each breast diagonally into 5 or 6 pieces.

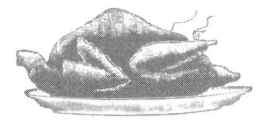

Quail with Cornbread Stuffing

Makes 6 servings

¼ cup vegetable oil
½ cup minced celery
¼ cup minced onion
2 cups crumbled cornbread or other day-old bread
¼ cup dried tart cherries
½ cup Chicken Stock (page 6)
2 tablespoons chopped flat-leaf parsley

¼ teaspoon ground coriander
½ teaspoon salt
¼ teaspoon freshly ground black pepper
¼ teaspoon ground nutmeg
6 quail, split down the backbone

Quail are small delicate game birds. This bird received its name from early colonists, who thought it was the same as a bird they knew back in Europe. But in truth the European quail is more of a migratory bird and is related to the partridge. Our quail aren't migratory at all—they nest on the ground and usually walk rather than fly. The meat of the American quail is not really gamy, although it also doesn't taste "just like chicken." It can be prepared by roasting, grilling, frying, or braising, and doesn't require a lot of cooking time. Because they are so small, you usually figure one bird per serving.

Sautéed greens or succotash with a thickened chicken stock would pair nicely with this dish.

* * *

Preheat the oven to 350°F. Lightly grease a 2-quart casserole dish and set aside.

Heat the oil in a medium skillet over medium heat. Add the celery and onion and cook, stirring, until the vegetables start to soften, 2 to 3 minutes. Add the bread crumbs and cherries, and stir. Add the stock and mix well. Add the parsley and spices. Mix well so all the ingredients come together. Check the seasoning and adjust if needed.

Spread half of the bread crumb mixture over the bottom of the prepared casserole dish. Add the quail, flesh side down. Spread the other half of the bread crumb mixture over the top. Place in the oven and bake for 15 to 20 minutes. The quail should be medium (pink inside). Cook a little longer for well-done.

Breaking Bread

Until the invention of the iron kitchen range at the turn of the 19th century, breads were baked in wood-fired brick ovens. Flour was stone-ground, and pearl ash was used as a rising agent, imparting a wonderful flavor to breads. Southerners used all sorts of grains to make bread, including white and yellow cornmeal and rice flour. No supper below the Mason–Dixon line was complete without cornbread. It was baked in an iron skillet, but like any favorite dish among a multicultural people, the exact ingredients varied considerably. Some recipes called for honey and fresh corn, which was absolutely eschewed in others. Another staple, hushpuppies, the accompaniment for fried fish, essentially used the same ingredients as cornbread—with a little onion and pepper—and then was fried.

Low-Country kitchens pretty much invented raised rice breads. The Carolina Housewife, published in 1847, contained no fewer than thirty recipes for rice breads. Aside from fried chicken, the buttermilk biscuit is the food most closely identified with the region. Southerners have long served biscuits—quick, easy, and inexpensive to make—at all times of day and with a variety of toppings. With a little sausage, ham, and gravy they become a hearty breakfast. Served plain, they are the requisite accompaniment for a meat or fowl supper. With homemade preserves, sour cream, or honey, the lowly buttermilk biscuit becomes a scrumptious snack.

Buttermilk Biscuits

Makes 12 to 14 biscuits

3¼ cups all-purpose flour
2¼ teaspoons baking powder
1½ teaspoons salt
¾ teaspoon baking soda

½ cup solid vegetable
   shortening, at room
   temperature
1½ cups buttermilk

A Southern staple, buttermilk biscuits are enjoyed at breakfast with homemade preserves or at supper dipped in a spicy Vegetable Gumbo (page 25) or Frogmore Stew (page 29). Kneading the dough with a machine tends to make it too tough. I find that using nature's tools, my own hands, works best.

* * *

Preheat the oven to 400°F. Line a baking sheet with baking parchment, or spray it with vegetable cooking spray.

In a large bowl, stir together the flour, baking powder, salt, and baking soda. Using your fingertips, work the shortening into the flour mixture for about 1 minute, or until well mixed. Add half of the buttermilk, and blend with your hands until the mixture resembles coarse crumbs. Add the remaining buttermilk and work it in until blended.

Lightly flour a smooth work surface. Using a floured rolling pin, roll out the dough so it is about ⁵⁄₁₆ inch thick. Using a 1- to 1½-inch round cutter or the top of a drinking glass, cut the dough into circles. Place them on the prepared baking sheet, leaving about ½ inch between circles. Bake for 20 to 25 minutes, or until golden brown.

Apple Bread

¾ cup firmly packed dark brown sugar
¼ cup vegetable oil
1 cup apple juice
1 large egg, at room temperature
2 cups all-purpose flour

1 tablespoon baking powder
1 teaspoon finely chopped fresh cilantro or 1 teaspoon ground coriander
½ teaspoon baking soda
½ teaspoon salt

Makes 1 loaf

This bread makes a good treat with coffee at any time of the day. It also freezes well.

* * *

Preheat the oven to 350°F. Spray the inside of a 10 × 5 × 3-inch loaf pan with vegetable cooking spray. (Or butter the pan, lightly dust it with flour, and tap out the excess.)

In a large bowl, using an electric mixer, cream the brown sugar and oil together. On low speed, add the apple juice and egg and beat just until combined.

In another large bowl, stir together the flour, baking powder, cilantro, baking soda, and salt. Make a well in the center of the flour mixture, add the apple juice mixture, and stir just until it is fully blended. Scrape the batter into the prepared pan. Bake for about 45 minutes, or until a toothpick inserted in the center of the bread comes out clean.

Remove the pan to a wire rack. Let it cool for 10 minutes before removing the bread from the pan; finish cooling the loaf on the rack. Cut the loaf into 10 to 12 slices. Store the completely cooled bread in an airtight container at room temperature.

Mango Coconut Muffins

Makes 12 muffins

1¾ cups all-purpose flour
¼ cup sugar
2 teaspoons baking powder
½ teaspoon salt
¾ cup fresh or canned
  unsweetened coconut milk

2 large eggs, at room
  temperature
3 tablespoons vegetable oil
1 cup ¼-inch pieces ripe mango
1 cup sweetened flaked coconut

These muffins work well for breakfast and brunch. For a great dessert, serve them with a scoop of ice cream and a touch of Crème Chantilly (page 190).

* * *

Preheat the oven to 350°F. Spray twelve 2½-inch muffin cups with vegetable cooking spray.

In a large bowl, stir together the flour, sugar, baking powder, and salt. In another bowl, stir together the coconut milk, eggs, and oil. Make a well in the center of the dry ingredients. Add the liquid ingredients and stir just to combine. Stir in the mango and coconut.

Spoon the batter into the prepared muffin cups. Bake for 20 to 25 minutes, or until a toothpick inserted in the center of a muffin comes out clean.

Remove the muffin tins to a wire rack. Let cool for 5 minutes before removing the muffins from the cups. Serve them piping hot, or finish cooling them on the rack. Store the completely cooled muffins in an airtight container at cool room temperature.

Sweet Potato Muffins

1¼ cups all-purpose flour
2 teaspoons baking powder
1 teaspoon baking soda
1 teaspoon ground cinnamon
⅛ teaspoon ground nutmeg
⅛ teaspoon ground ginger
½ teaspoon salt
1 cup mashed Baked Sweet
  Potatoes (page 108)

1 cup firmly packed dark brown
  sugar
½ cup (1 stick) unsalted butter,
  melted and cooled
2 large eggs, at room
  temperature
1 teaspoon vanilla extract
¾ cup golden raisins
½ cup sunflower seeds

Makes 16 muffins

* * *

This bread is versatile enough to serve at brunch and dinner. It isn't all that sweet, and it makes a nice change from the ordinary muffin.

* * *

Preheat the oven to 400°F. Spray sixteen 2½-inch muffin cups with vegetable cooking spray.

Into a large bowl, sift together the flour, baking powder, baking soda, cinnamon, nutmeg, ginger, and salt. In another bowl, whisk together the sweet potatoes, brown sugar, butter, eggs, and vanilla until blended. With your hand, toss the raisins and sunflower seeds into the flour mixture. Make a well in the center of the dry ingredients. Add the sweet potato mixture and stir just to combine.

Spoon the batter into the prepared muffin cups. Bake for 15 to 20 minutes, or until a toothpick inserted in the center of a muffin comes out clean.

Remove the muffin tins to a wire rack. Let cool for 5 to 8 minutes before removing the muffins from the cups. Serve them piping hot with butter, jam, or honey, or finish cooling them on the rack. Store completely cooled muffins in an airtight container at cool room temperature.

Herbed Potato Bread

Makes 3 loaves

2 cups milk
2 Idaho potatoes
3 cups lukewarm water
   (105° to 115°F)
2 packages active dry yeast
2 tablespoons granulated sugar
3 tablespoons vegetable oil
3 tablespoons chopped onion
1 tablespoon celery seeds

2½ teaspoons dried savory leaves
1 tablespoon salt
2 teaspoons freshly ground black
   pepper
2 cloves Roasted Garlic
   (page 73), pressed through a
   garlic press
8 cups all-purpose flour

When you think of comfort food, the potato in some shape or form comes to mind. There is nothing more comforting than the aroma of this wonderful herby bread as it is baking. This recipe makes three loaves because it calls for a potato starter, which needs a certain amount of each ingredient to get it to work properly; note that you'll need three loaf pans. The bread tastes great the next day, toasted and spread with butter. If three loaves seems like a lot, you can always freeze a loaf or two once they have cooled down.

* * *

Heat the milk in a saucepan over medium heat just until it starts to boil. Remove the pan from the heat and set it aside to cool.

Peel the potatoes and cut them into 1- to 2-inch chunks. Put the potatoes in a medium saucepan, add the water, and place over high heat. Bring the mixture to a boil. Boil for about 20 minutes, or until the potatoes are soft when pierced with the point of a sharp knife. Drain the potatoes, reserving 1 cup of the cooking water. Mash the potatoes and reserve 1 cup. (Save any extra for another use.)

Pour the reserved cooking water into a large bowl. Sprinkle in the yeast and sugar, and stir until the yeast is dissolved.

Let stand for about 5 minutes. Stir in the mashed potatoes, the cooled milk, and the oil, onion, celery seeds, savory, salt, pepper, and garlic. Stir in 4 cups of the flour until well combined. Mix in enough of the remaining flour to make a firm dough that pulls away from the sides of the bowl. Turn the dough out onto a lightly floured work surface and knead for 10 to 15 minutes, or until the dough is smooth and elastic.

Shape the dough into a ball and place it in an oiled bowl, turning it to grease the dough all over. Cover with a clean cloth and let rise in a warm, draft-free place until doubled in bulk, 1 to 1½ hours. Lightly oil three 9 × 5 × 3-inch loaf pans or spray them with vegetable cooking spray.

Punch the dough down and divide it into 3 equal pieces. Shape each piece into a loaf, and place each one in a prepared loaf pan. Cover and let rise again until doubled in bulk, about 1½ hours.

Toward the end of the rising time, preheat the oven to 350°F.

Bake the loaves for 40 to 45 minutes, or until well browned and hollow-sounding when tapped. Turn them out of the pans and cool them, right side up, on a wire rack before slicing.

Sage and Cheese Biscuits

Makes about 19 biscuits

Sage leaves are slightly fuzzy, grayish green, elongated ovals. Sage has a sort of earthy smell and taste. It's used a lot in sausages and pork dishes.

½ cup whole-wheat flour
1½ cups all-purpose flour
¼ cup shredded sharp cheddar cheese
¼ cup shredded pepper Jack cheese or your favorite spicy cheese

1 tablespoon baking powder
2 teaspoons finely chopped fresh sage leaves
5 tablespoons solid vegetable shortening
½ to ¾ cup buttermilk

These add a little something extra to the classic Southern biscuit. You can serve them with butter straight out of the oven. You can also make them larger and use them for sandwiches, such as chicken, pork, or catfish. These biscuits fit in with just about anything you might serve another bread with.

* * *

Preheat the oven to 450°F. Spray a baking sheet with vegetable cooking spray or lightly brush the sheet with vegetable oil.

In a large bowl, stir together the flours, cheeses, baking powder, and sage. Add the shortening and using your fingertips, quickly rub the shortening into the flour mixture until combined. Mix in ½ cup of the buttermilk. Add more buttermilk if necessary to get the ingredients to form a dough.

Lightly flour a work surface with all-purpose flour. Dump the dough onto the work surface and gently knead it until it is one smooth ball.

Using a lightly floured rolling pin, roll the dough out to ½-inch thickness. Using a floured 2-inch cookie cutter or drinking glass, cut out biscuits from the dough. Place the biscuits on the prepared baking sheet and bake for 10 to 12 minutes, or until they are golden brown. Serve warm.

Cornbread

½ cup coarse yellow cornmeal
1½ cups all-purpose flour
⅓ cup firmly packed light
   brown sugar
1 teaspoon baking powder
¼ teaspoon baking soda

½ teaspoon salt
½ teaspoon ground coriander
1½ cups buttermilk
1 large egg, lightly beaten
¼ cup vegetable oil

Makes 10 servings

Variation
Stir in ⅓ cup corn kernels
or ⅓ cup chopped roasted
red pepper, if desired.

No Southern meal is complete without cornbread. Traditionally cornbread is baked in an iron skillet, but a baking pan works too. As with many favorite Southern recipes, the recipes vary from family to family. Some call for honey, sugar, fresh corn kernels, and other ingredients such as peppers. I suggest trial-and-error testing (starting with this recipe first, of course!) until you find the version that you like best.

* * *

Preheat the oven to 375°F. Lightly oil a 10-inch iron skillet or baking pan, or spray with vegetable cooking spray.

In a large bowl, mix together the cornmeal, flour, brown sugar, baking powder, baking soda, salt, and coriander.

Stir in the buttermilk, egg, and oil until the mixture is smooth. Pour the batter into the prepared skillet or baking pan. Bake for 40 minutes or until the cornbread is golden brown and dry in the center.

The Southerner's Sweet Tooth

The Southerner's sweet tooth reached its apotheosis in Charleston and Savannah in the 17th and 18th centuries. Not only did residents have access to abundant sugar but they were exposed to exotic fruits like bananas and coconuts. The Low-Country kitchen was a cornucopia of confectionery delights. My good friend Cynthia Long and I have created a contemporary dessert menu in this chapter. Standards like mud pie, carrot cake, and bread pudding are invigorated with new ingredients. Enjoy!

Sweet Potato Crème Brûlée

Makes 8 servings

1½ pounds sweet potatoes,
baked, peeled, and pureed
(page 108)
2½ cups granulated sugar

1 tablespoon fresh lemon juice
2 quarts heavy cream
1 vanilla bean, split in half
16 large egg yolks

One of the many challenges of being a culinary artist is knowing that nothing under the sun hasn't been done already (or has it?). In the case of this recipe, the "new" comes from the unique fusion of sweet potatoes into this classic dessert. The satisfying flavor of sweet potatoes is a natural with cool, smooth crème brûlée.

The literal translation of *crème brûlée* is "burnt cream." Actually it is a chilled custard that is sprinkled with granulated or brown sugar. It is then heated under the broiler until the sugar caramelizes and forms a brittle topping.

❉   ❉   ❉

In a medium bowl, mix together the pureed sweet potatoes, ¼ cup of the sugar, and the lemon juice until combined. Butter eight 8-ounce custard cups or ramekins. Spoon 2 to 3 tablespoons of the sweet potato mixture into each cup to form a ¼-inch-thick layer.

Preheat the oven to 325°F.

In a medium saucepan, combine the heavy cream, vanilla bean, and ¾ cup of the remaining sugar. Bring the mixture to a boil over medium heat. Remove the pan from the heat.

In a large bowl, whisk together the egg yolks and another ¾ cup sugar. Gradually pour the egg mixture into the saucepan, whisking constantly. Return the saucepan to the stove and cook on low heat for 3 minutes, or until the mixture thickens.

Fill the custard cups with enough of the cream mixture so they are about seven-eighths full. Place the filled cups in a baking pan that is large enough to hold them all. Add enough hot water to come within 1 inch of the top of the cups. Bake for 45 minutes, or until the custards are barely set and a toothpick inserted into the center comes out a little wet. Remove the custards from the baking pan and place them in the refrigerator. Refrigerate overnight.

Preheat the broiler. Lightly sprinkle the surface of each custard with 1½ tablespoons of the remaining sugar. Place the custards under the broiler for about 30 to 60 seconds and let them brown. Keep an eye on the custards, as this happens quickly.

Remove the custards from the heat, and once the sugar has hardened (1 to 2 minutes), serve the Crème Brûlée.

Citrus Pound Cake

Makes 8 to 10 servings

¾ cup (1½ sticks) unsalted butter, softened
¾ cup granulated sugar
Juice of 1 orange
Juice of 1 lemon
Juice of 1 lime
1½ teaspoons vanilla extract

3 large eggs
2¾ cups all-purpose flour
1½ teaspoons baking powder
Pinch of salt
Confectioners' sugar, for dusting (optional)

The basic recipe for pound cake used to call for a pound of butter, a pound of eggs, a pound of sugar, a pound of flour, and a shot of vanilla, thus resulting in its appropriate name. We added a little fresh citrus juice to the recipe to give it a refreshing revamping.

Pound cake is one of those desserts you can serve in many ways. You can serve it hot, warm, or cold. Crème Chantilly (page 190), ice cream, fresh fruit (such as Drunken Strawberries, page 185), and chocolate sauce are just a few great topping ideas.

* * *

Preheat the oven to 350°F. Butter a 9-inch-diameter Bundt pan.

In a large bowl, using an electric mixer set on medium speed, cream together the butter and sugar until the mixture is light and fluffy, about 5 minutes. Beat in the 3 juices and the vanilla. One at a time, beat in the eggs, beating well after each addition.

In another mixing bowl, sift together the flour, baking powder, and salt. Stir the flour mixture into the batter until combined. Scrape the mixture into the prepared pan and bake for 40 to 45 minutes, or until a toothpick inserted in the center of the cake comes out clean. Transfer the Bundt pan to a wire rack and let it cool for 10 minutes. Then turn the cake out of the pan and let it cool completely on the rack. Dust the top with confectioners' sugar, if desired, just before serving.

Drunken Strawberries

1½ pints ripe strawberries, washed, hulled, and sliced in half
¼ cup dark brown sugar

¼ cup bourbon
1 teaspoon vanilla extract
½ teaspoon fresh lemon juice

Makes about 4 cups, or 6 servings

This is a nice summer treat that can be eaten with Crème Chantilly (page 190) or Citrus Pound Cake (page 184), or simply by itself.

* * *

Mix all of the ingredients in a bowl and chill before using. If you have any left over, store them in an airtight container in the refrigerator for up to a week.

My Favorite Mini Mud Pies

Makes 12 servings

1½ cups all-purpose flour
¾ cup granulated sugar
¾ cup firmly packed light
  brown sugar
¾ teaspoon baking soda
½ teaspoon ground mace
½ teaspoon ground cinnamon
¼ teaspoon salt
¾ cup water
¼ cup (½ stick) unsalted butter
¼ cup solid vegetable
  shortening

¼ cup unsweetened cocoa
  powder
¼ cup heavy cream
1 large egg
1 tablespoon Kahlúa
About 1½ cups Ganache
  (page 193)
¼ cup miniature semisweet
  chocolate chips
¼ cup sweetened flaked coconut
  (optional)
¼ cup chopped pecans

Some of you may not have tasted or even heard of a Mud Pie, so you might wonder, how can this possibly taste good with a name like Mud Pie? I am truly a chocolate-lover, and if you are anything like me, then I guarantee you will be blown away by this dessert. It's rich, dark, and full of chocolate—which is how the pie got its name. This recipe was created by one of the best pastry chefs around, my good friend and colleague Cynthia Long. You can serve this pie hot, warm, or cold, and it goes really well with whipped cream and/or ice cream.

* * *

Preheat the oven to 400°F. Lightly oil 12 standard-size muffin cups and dust them with flour.

In a medium bowl, stir together the flour, sugars, baking soda, mace, cinnamon, and salt to combine.

In a medium saucepan, combine the water, butter, shortening, and cocoa powder and cook over medium heat until the mixture comes to a boil. Remove the mixture from the heat and scrape it into a large bowl. Stir in the flour mixture until well combined. Add the cream, egg, and Kahlúa, stirring until all the ingredients are thoroughly combined.

Divide the batter evenly among the prepared muffin cups. Bake for 10 to 15 minutes, or until a toothpick inserted into the center of one "pie" comes out clean. Remove the pans to a wire rack and let them cool for 30 minutes. Remove the pies from the muffin cups and cool completely on the rack.

Frost each pie with Ganache, and sprinkle the top of each one with chocolate chips, coconut, if using, and pecans.

Praline Bread Pudding

Makes 10 servings

Note: To roast pecans and other nuts, preheat the oven to 375°F and arrange the nuts in a single layer on a baking sheet. Place the sheet in the oven and roast until the nuts become golden brown, 5 to 6 minutes. Watch carefully to make sure the nuts don't burn. Store in an airtight container at room temperature for up to 2 weeks.

For the Praline
2 cups granulated sugar
½ cup water
½ cup (1 stick) unsalted butter
½ cup heavy cream
2 cups pecan halves, roasted (see Note)

For the bread pudding
6 large egg yolks
3 cups heavy cream
3 cups milk
1 cup firmly packed light brown sugar
¾ cup bourbon
1 vanilla bean, split lengthwise
½ cup golden raisins (not necessary if using raisin bread)
2½ pounds challah, raisin, or brioche bread, cut into 1-inch pieces

Praline is a confection made from almonds or pecans and caramel. This particular dessert is of French descent, but it has a very Southern character as well. It was and is a big dish in Creole-style cooking, which boasts the influences of France, Spain, and the Caribbean. In the Creole kitchen, pecans are used. Praline is said to have gotten its name from a French diplomat, César du Plessis–Praslin, and was first mentioned in print in 1727. It was considered a culinary staple in New Orleans by 1762.

* * *

To make the praline, line a baking sheet with baking parchment or lightly oil the sheet. In a medium-size heavy saucepan, stir together the sugar and water. Cook over medium heat, stirring constantly, until the sugar dissolves. Increase the heat to high and bring the mixture to a boil. Reduce the heat to low and continue to cook until the mixture becomes golden brown, about 7 to 10 minutes. Remove the pan from the heat and then whisk in the butter. Immediately whisk in the cream. Stir in the pecans and pour the mixture on the prepared baking sheet. Set aside and cool completely. When it is cool, break the praline into ¼- to ½-inch pieces.

Preheat the oven to 350°F. Lightly butter a 9-inch square baking dish.

To make the custard for the bread pudding, place the egg yolks in a medium bowl and lightly whisk together. In a medium saucepan, combine the heavy cream, milk, brown sugar, bourbon, and vanilla bean. Bring the mixture to a boil over medium heat. Remove the pan from the heat. Set aside and let cool to 80°F (warm to the touch when tested with your fingertip). Whisk the eggs into the mixture.

Scatter over the bottom of the prepared baking dish, then the raisins (if using), and half of the bread, then half of the praline. Repeat the layers. Pour the custard mixture over the top. Bake for 50 to 60 minutes, or until a knife inserted into the center of the pudding comes out clean.

Crème Chantilly

Makes about 2 cups

2 cups heavy cream, chilled
¼ cup confectioners' sugar

1 tablespoon vanilla extract

This sweetened whipped cream is good for a multitude of uses. Try it as a topping for fresh fruit, such as strawberries, or as a filler for shortcake.

* * *

Combine all the ingredients in a bowl. Using an electric mixer, whip until the cream is just stiff. (Do not whip too much or the cream will break.)

The Killer Chocolate Cake

3 cups cake flour
1 teaspoon baking soda
1 teaspoon salt
¼ teaspoon ground cinnamon
2 cups granulated sugar
1 cup solid vegetable shortening
3 ounces unsweetened chocolate,
 melted and cooled

1 teaspoon vanilla extract
1 teaspoon bourbon
3 large eggs
1 cup buttermilk
1 recipe Ganache
 (recipe follows)

Makes one 9-inch round
layer cake

Chocolate comes from a tropical bean (cacao). The beans are fermented, then dried and roasted. After that process they are cracked to separate the outer shell from the core. The core is then ground to extract a thick brown paste, called the liquor. Milk, vanilla, and sugar are added to the liquor to make such products as semisweet and sweet chocolate. Baking chocolate contains no sugar.

Making chocolate from scratch is probably not something that is on your priority list, but the next time you need to fulfill that chocolate craving, here is *the* killer chocolate cake recipe for you. Serve it with a tall glass of cold milk.

*   *   *

Preheat the oven to 350°F. Spray two 9-inch round baking pans with vegetable cooking spray. (Or grease with solid vegetable shortening and dust lightly with flour, tapping out any excess.)

In a mixing bowl, sift together the flour, baking soda, salt, and cinnamon.

In a large bowl, using an electric mixer, cream together the sugar and shortening until light and fluffy. Beat in the chocolate, vanilla, and bourbon. One at a time, beat in the eggs, beating well after each addition.

continued

In three additions each, beat in the flour mixture and the buttermilk, scraping down the sides of the bowl after each addition. Divide the batter evenly between the 2 prepared pans. Bake for 30 to 40 minutes or until a toothpick inserted into the center of each cake comes out clean. Remove the pans to a wire rack and let cool for 10 minutes. Remove the cakes from the pans and cool completely on the rack.

Frost each of the cakes with some of the Ganache. Place the cakes in the refrigerator for about 1 hour to let the Ganache set. Remove the cakes from the refrigerator and stack one cake on top of the other. Hide the joining of the two cakes with more of the Ganache. Apply another thin layer of Ganache on top of cake to ensure a smooth surface.

Ganache

2½ cups heavy cream
¼ cup granulated sugar
¼ cup (½ stick) unsalted butter,
  softened

20 ounces (2½ cups) chopped
  semisweet chocolate or
  semisweet chocolate chips

Makes about 4½ cups

Ganache is a rich chocolate icing made of semisweet chocolate and whipping cream. They are heated and stirred together until the chocolate has melted. Then the mixture is cooled and poured over cakes or other pastries. To make a rich chocolate fudge sauce, heat the ganache to melt it. Or stir some ganache into hot milk for a killer hot chocolate.

* * *

In a medium saucepan, combine the cream, sugar, and butter. Heat the ganache over low heat to melt it. Remove the pan from the heat. Add the chocolate and stir until the chocolate is melted. Let the ganache cool until thick enough to spread over cakes or pastries. If cooled too long, it could firm up too much. Cover and refrigerate the leftovers.

Bourbon Truffles

1 cup heavy cream
10 ounces semisweet chocolate,
  finely chopped

¼ cup bourbon
About ⅓ cup unsweetened
  cocoa powder

Truffles are made by combining melted chocolate with various ingredients or flavorings such as liqueurs, coffee, or nuts. Then the mixture is cooled until it can be shaped into balls. They are then dusted with cocoa powder, or covered with nuts or sprinkles. But of course you can just leave the outside plain.

* * *

In a medium-size heavy saucepan over low heat, bring the cream to a slow boil. Add the chocolate and remove the pan from the heat. Let stand for 2 to 3 minutes. Whisk in the bourbon until the chocolate is blended into the cream. Scrape the mixture into a shallow dish and refrigerate until the mixture is firm, 30 to 60 minutes.

Place the cocoa powder in a small bowl. Using a small ice cream scoop or melon baller, scoop the chocolate mixture into small balls and drop them into the cocoa powder. Roll the truffles in the cocoa powder to evenly coat them. Place the truffles in a single layer in an airtight container. Refrigerate until firm.

Before serving, let the truffles stand at room temperature for 15 to 20 minutes.

Pecan Pie

Pastry for 1 pie crust
1½ cups pecan halves
4 large eggs
½ cup granulated sugar
½ cup firmly packed light brown
  sugar
½ cup molasses

½ cup dark corn syrup
¼ cup (½ stick) unsalted butter,
  melted
½ teaspoon vanilla extract
⅛ teaspoon salt
1 tablespoon all-purpose flour

Makes 8 servings

Everybody who enjoys Southern-style foods loves this favorite. A bit of molasses gives this version a deeper, less cloying flavor than other recipes. Ice cream or whipped cream adds the final touch.

*　*　*

Preheat the oven to 375°F. Fit the pastry into a 9-inch pie plate. Sprinkle the pecans over the pastry.

In a large bowl, using an electric mixer set on medium-high speed, beat the eggs until they form a thin ribbon when the beaters are lifted. Add the sugars and mix thoroughly. Gradually add the molasses and corn syrup. Beat in the butter, vanilla, and salt. Whisk in the flour. Pour the mixture over the nuts in the pie crust. Bake for 1 hour, or until the filling is puffy and the crust is golden. Serve warm or cold.

Carrot Cake

Makes one 9-inch
square cake, or
8 servings

1½ cups sifted all-purpose flour
½ cup granulated sugar
½ cup firmly packed light brown
   sugar
1 teaspoon baking powder
1 teaspoon baking soda
1 teaspoon ground cinnamon
¼ teaspoon ground nutmeg
½ teaspoon salt
2 large eggs
⅔ cup canola oil

½ cup grated carrot
½ cup canned crushed pineapple
   with juice
½ cup golden raisins
¼ cup freshly grated coconut or
   unsweetened flaked coconut
2 teaspoons vanilla extract
1 recipe Cream Cheese Frosting
   (recipe follows), or
   confectioners' sugar for
   dusting (optional)

Carrot cake is one of those recipes that is ever changing. I've seen it with frosting, without frosting, with and without nuts, with different kinds of dried fruits such as cherries, figs, and apricots. Here's my take on this favorite cake. I've added freshly grated coconut to give it a sweet nuttiness, but for convenience you can substitute unsweetened flakes.

* * *

Preheat the oven to 350°F. Spray a 9-inch square baking pan with vegetable cooking spray and dust it with flour.

In a medium bowl, stir together the flour, sugars, baking powder, baking soda, cinnamon, nutmeg, and salt. In a large bowl, whisk together the eggs and oil. Add the egg mixture to the flour ingredients and stir until combined. Stir in the carrots, pineapple, raisins, coconut, and vanilla until combined.

Scrape the batter into the prepared pan. Bake for 35 to 40 minutes, or until a toothpick inserted into the center of the cake comes out clean. Remove the pan to a wire rack and let it cool for 15 minutes. Remove the cake from the pan, and frost it with Cream Cheese Frosting or dust it with confectioners' sugar, if desired.

Cream Cheese Frosting

8 ounces cream cheese, softened
¼ cup (½ stick) unsalted butter, softened
1 teaspoon vanilla extract

3 cups sifted confectioners' sugar
3 ounces white chocolate, melted and cooled

Makes frosting for one 2-layer 9-inch cake

The addition of white chocolate to this classic recipe adds a little depth and complexity to the flavor as well as making the spread creamier. It's perfect with Carrot Cake.

* * *

In a large bowl, using an electric mixer on medium speed, cream together the cream cheese, butter, and vanilla until combined. Gradually add the confectioners' sugar until combined. Beat in the white chocolate. (If the frosting seems to be a little thick, thin it with a touch of milk.) This will keep for 1 week in a covered container in the refrigerator.

Spiced Apple Cobbler

Makes about 9 servings

For the pastry crust
3 cups all-purpose flour
2 tablespoons granulated sugar
2 teaspoons baking powder
1 teaspoon salt
½ cup (1 stick) unsalted butter
½ cup solid vegetable shortening
10 tablespoons ice-cold water

For the filling
3½ pounds Granny Smith apples, peeled, cored, and cut into ¼-inch slices

1 cup firmly packed dark brown sugar
2 tablespoons cornstarch
2 teaspoons ground cinnamon
¼ teaspoon ground mace
¼ teaspoon ground nutmeg
¼ cup orange juice

For the topping
1 large egg
½ teaspoon milk
2 tablespoons granulated sugar

Cobblers come in a variety of flavors and styles. There is a debate about whether the topping should be biscuit, pastry, or crumb. My vote is for pastry on the bottom and the top. Give this recipe a try and see if you agree.

* * *

To make the pastry crust, sift the flour, sugar, baking powder, and salt together into a large bowl. Cut the butter into ½-inch cubes and distribute them over the flour mixture. With a pastry blender or two knives used in scissors-like fashion, cut in the butter and the shortening, small amounts at a time, until the mixture resembles cornmeal. Sprinkle the water over the mixture. Using your fingertips, blend with your fingers until combined. Divide the pastry mixture in half and shape each half into a disk. Wrap, and let rest in the refrigerator until ready to use.

To make the apple filling, combine all of the filling ingredients in a large saucepan over low heat. Cook, stirring occasionally, until the apples start to soften, 8 to 10 minutes. Let cool.

Preheat the oven to 400°F.

On a lightly floured work surface, using a lightly floured rolling pin, roll one of the disks to form a 12-inch square. Transfer the dough to a 9-inch square baking pan. Place the apple filling in the crust. Roll out the remaining disk to form a square that is a large enough to cover the apples. Place this dough on top of the apples and pinch the edges of the top and bottom pastries together to seal.

Whisk together the egg and milk until blended. Using a pastry brush, brush the pastry with this egg wash. Sprinkle the 2 table-spoons granulated sugar evenly over the top. Using the point of a sharp knife, make several cuts through the top of the pastry. Bake for 25 to 35 minutes, or until the pastry is golden brown and the filling is bubbling.

Sweet Potato Granny Smith Pear Stack

5 sweet potatoes, peeled

6 Granny Smith pears, cored and peeled

1½ tablespoons Marv's Sweet Spice (page 65), or 1 teaspoon ground cinnamon plus 1 teaspoon ground nutmeg plus 2 teaspoons dark brown sugar

1 teaspoon honey

¼ teaspoon fresh lemon juice

Once again, here's the sweet potato in a dessert recipe. The pear that I have selected for this recipe, the Granny Smith pear, has a firmness that is perfect for baking. Combined, these two form a winning duo. If Granny Smith pears are unavailable, substitute Comice pears. It is thought that the pear originated in Asia, possibly China, and has been cultivated since at least 2000 B.C., with more than 5,000 species. Most American varieties come from a European version that was brought to this country in the 17th century. As with other fruits that were introduced to the South, they were often pickled or canned.

Serve these with ice cream or whipped cream.

* * *

Preheat the oven to 350°F.

Using a mandoline or a very sharp knife, slice the sweet potatoes and the pears into ½-inch-thick rounds. Place a slice of sweet potato on a baking sheet. Sprinkle it with a little of the Marv's Sweet Spice. Top it with a pear slice and sprinkle with a little more of the spice. Repeat until you have about 5 layers. Repeat with the remaining fruit and spice. Bake the stacks for 25 to 30 minutes, or until tender.

Remove them from the oven and let cool for 10 minutes. This will allow the sugar to harden and the layers to seal together. Mix the honey and lemon juice together, and drizzle the mixture over the top of the baked stacks. The stacks can be eaten hot, warm, or cold.

Gingersnap Cookies

Makes about 20 cookies

1 cup all-purpose flour
2½ tablespoons granulated sugar
1 tablespoon ground ginger
¼ teaspoon baking soda
Pinch of salt
½ cup molasses

¼ cup dark corn syrup
10 tablespoons (1¼ sticks)
   unsalted butter
1 large egg
1 tablespoon grated fresh ginger
1 teaspoon vanilla extract

Ginger is a native of tropical and subtropical regions. It used to be primarily from Asia until Marco Polo brought it back from his expedition. It is said that Queen Elizabeth I of England loved the spice so much she invented the gingerbread-man cookie. The English brought it to America, supposedly to Virginia. It is said that ginger was being used in the Low Country as early as the mid 1600s in chutneys and marinades, as well as desserts. I like to serve these thin, crisp cookies with a glass of milk or a dish of vanilla ice cream.

* * *

Preheat the oven to 375°F. Lightly butter two baking sheets.

In a mixing bowl, sift together the flour, sugar, ground ginger, baking soda, and salt.

In a medium saucepan over medium-high heat, bring the molasses and corn syrup to a boil. Continue to boil until the mixture is reduced a little and starts to thicken, 5 to 7 minutes. Stir in the butter and cook 1 minute longer. Remove the saucepan from the heat and let the mixture cool to lukewarm. Then stir in the egg, fresh ginger, and vanilla. Stir the flour mixture into the molasses mixture until combined. The batter will be loose.

Using a tablespoon, drop the batter onto the prepared baking sheets, leaving about 3 inches between cookies. Bake for 5 to

6 minutes, rotating the baking sheets halfway through the baking time to ensure even browning.

Remove the baking sheets to wire racks and let them cool for 1 minute. Using a metal spatula, transfer the cookies to wire racks and cool completely. (If you like soft cookies, simply preheat the oven to 350°F, put some cooled cookies on a baking sheet, and place in the oven until warm, 1 to 2 minutes.) Store the cookies in an airtight container at room temperature for up to 2 weeks.

Refreshing and Relaxing Beverages

In this chapter we have several Southern staples. Some are alcohol-based and some are not. In any case some of these drinks are cool and refreshing on a hot summer day, and others can help you unwind from just a long day in general. Some of the recipes can be used as a base for experimentation—try them as they are, then feel free to improvise. The end result will always quench a thirst.

Iced Tea

Makes 4 to 6 servings

6 to 8 tea bags
6 cups boiling water
¼ cup fresh lemon juice
    (optional)

¼ cup granulated sugar
    (optional)

Did you know that iced tea was born at the 1904 St. Louis World's Fair? How it became one of the South's most celebrated drinks isn't really known. It can be made in several ways. Whether you like it with or without lemon and sugar is completely up to you. Use this recipe as is, or use it as a base, adding or omitting what you like. Never chill iced tea in the refrigerator, or it will get cloudy.

* * *

Place the tea bags in a large heatproof pitcher. Pour the boiling water over the tea bags. Let stand for 3 to 5 minutes, or longer for stronger tea. Remove the tea bags. Add the lemon, if desired. Stir in the sugar, if desired, until dissolved. Let cool. Pour over ice and serve.

Made-from-Scratch Lemonade

2 quarts water
Juice of 6 lemons
Juice of 2 oranges
Juice of 1 lime

1 cup granulated sugar (give or take a little, according to your preference)

Makes 2¾ quarts, or 8 servings

There's just nothing like the real thing!

* * *

Mix all the ingredients together in a pitcher. Stir until the sugar dissolves. Serve in chilled glasses filled with ice.

Lou's Lemon Comfort Deluxe

Makes 4 servings

Note: Don't overstir after you add the sparkling water. The bubbles aerate the drink and make it light and refreshing.

¾ cups Made-from-Scratch Lemonade (page 207)
¼ cup chilled Southern Comfort
½ cup chilled champagne

¼ cup chilled sparkling water
Twist of lemon and/or a sprig of fresh mint, for garnish (optional)

A good friend of mine and a terrific bartender, Lou Canteres, whipped this drink up for us one hot, humid July night. When the heat is on, make up a few of these and you won't even notice.

* * *

Pour the Made-from-Scratch Lemonade into a chilled pitcher. Add the Southern Comfort and champagne and stir. Top with the sparkling water and give a couple of stirs more. Pour into tall glasses and add a lemon twist or mint sprig, if desired.

Mint Julep

1 large bunch fresh mint (dried mint won't do here)
2 cups finely crushed ice
4 to 6 ounces bourbon (1 ounce per glass)

4 to 6 tablespoons Simple Syrup (recipe follows; 1 tablespoon per glass)
½ to ¾ cup sparkling water (2 tablespoons per glass)

Makes 4 to 6 servings

This drink is a favorite throughout the South. It is believed that the Mint Julep originated in Kentucky, and it is certainly synonymous with the famous Kentucky Derby. Don't wait for the next Derby to come around before you experience how refreshing and good this drink is. Try it out on the next hot day.

* * *

Place 10 to 12 mint leaves in the bottom of each glass. Place 2 to 3 tablespoons of crushed ice on top. Using a mortar or a wooden spoon, mash the ice into the mint for 30 to 40 seconds. Add the bourbon, Simple Syrup, and sparkling water. Stir. Garnish with a fresh mint sprig and serve.

Simple Syrup (Sugar Syrup)

Makes 1½ cups

1 cup water

½ cup granulated sugar

Simple Syrup can be used for anything from poaching fruit, soaking cakes, and glazing baked goods to flavoring mixed drinks. It is basically a way of adding sweetness to recipes without having to worry about sugar crystals not dissolving.

* * *

In a small saucepan, heat the water and sugar together over low heat until the syrup becomes clear, 5 to 7 minutes. Remove from the heat, let cool, and use, or store in an airtight container in the refrigerator for up to 2 weeks.

The Old Fashioned

1 orange slice
1 maraschino cherry
3 dashes of Angostura bitters or orange bitters
2 to 3 ounces sparkling water (optional)

1 teaspoon Simple Syrup (page 210)
3 to 4 tablespoons crushed ice
2 ounces bourbon

Makes 1 cocktail

This is one of those examples of which came first, the chicken or the egg, stories. This drink gets its name from the glass called the old-fashioned. But it is also reported that the drink came first, and that the glass was developed to accommodate the large amount of ingredients.

* * *

In a tall glass (a double old-fashioned glass if you have one), combine the orange slice, cherry, bitters, sparkling water, if using, and Simple Syrup. Using a mortar or a wooden spoon, mash the ingredients until they start to blend together. Fill the glass three-quarters full with ice. Add the bourbon, stir gently, and serve.

Whiskey Sour

Makes 1 cocktail

2 ounces bourbon
½ cup freshly made lemonade

1 orange slice

The whiskey sour gets its name from its sharp, tart taste. This drink is pretty versatile. First, it can be shaken (made with ice and then strained out) or stirred (made with ice left in). Second, it can be served cool, on the rocks (poured over ice), or straight up (made at room temperature and served with no ice). It can also be made with several other liquors if you do not like whiskey. You can use bourbon, gin, or rum.

* * *

Combine all of the ingredients in a cocktail shaker or stir in a large glass. As explained in the headnote, this can be served at room temperature, or cool, over ice or straight up.

Index

catfish:
    pan-fried, 120–21
    in seafood gumbo, 26–27
celeriac puree, 112
cheese:
    macaroni and, 94
    and sage biscuits, 178
    see also mascarpone cheese
cherry:
    chutney, sweet and tart, 80
    and pineapple chutney, 78
chicken:
    burner's barbecue, 159
    country captain, 162–63
    Creole braised, with golden rice, 161
    gingersnap-braised, 160
    home-style smothered, 164
    roasted, 158
    in roasted farm-raised guinea hen, 165
    and sausage gumbo, 28
    Southern-exposed fried, 154–55
    stewed, 156–57
    stock, 6
chicken-fried steak, 139
chicken livers, sautéed, 43
    in dirty rice, 89
chili paste, 70
    in bourbon-cured salmon, 122
    in bourbon-soaked pork chops, 140
    in Creole sauce, 12–13
    in grilled filet mignon with brown oyster gravy, 149–50
    in Marv's hot sauce, 67
    in pickled okra, 68–69
    in spicy pulled pork shoulder, 142–43

chili rub, 75
chocolate:
    in bourbon truffles, 194
    cake, the killer, 191–92
    in ganache, 193
    in my favorite mini mud pies, 186–87
chutneys:
    pineapple and cherry, 78
    sweet and tart cherry, 80
    tropical fruit, 79
circuit hash, 97
    lentil lima bean, 104–5
citrus pound cake, 184
cocktail sauce, 37
    in shrimp cocktail, 36
coconut:
    in carrot cake, 196
    mango muffins, 174
    rice, 91
cod, in seafood gumbo, 26–27
cold vegetable soup, 31
cole slaw, 54
collard greens, sautéed, 98–99
colombo-dusted sea scallops, 130
condiments, 63–80
    blackened red pepper spread, 77
    bread-n-butter pickle mayonnaise, 71
    chili paste, 70
    chili rub, 75
    Marv's bay spice, 66
    Marv's garlic rub, 76
    Marv's hot sauce, 67
    Marv spice (savory), 64
    Marv's sweet spice, 65
    pickled okra, 68–69
    roasted garlic and garlic oil, 73
    roasted shallots, 74

gravies (*continued*)

    pan, 18

    roasted shallot pan, 148

green bell peppers, *see* pepper(s)

grilled filet mignon with brown oyster gravy, 149–50

grits, yellow hominy, 93

guava, in tropical fruit chutney, 79

guinea hen, roasted farm-raised, 165

gumbos, 12

    chicken and sausage, 28

    monkfish and sweet sausage, 131

    seafood, 26–27

    vegetable, 25

Ham, in macaroni salad, 57

haricots verts, in baby green beans, 101

herbed potato bread, 176–77

herb vinaigrette, 53

    wilted greens with, 52–53

home-style smothered chicken, 164

honey-orange-glazed grilled Muscovy duck breast, 166–67

hoppin' John, 83

hushpuppies, 42

Iced tea, 206

Kale, 97

in five-greens rice, 86

in Frogmore stew, 29–30

in wilted greens with herb vinaigrette, 52–53

killer chocolate cake, the, 191–92

Leek asparagus soup, 23

lemon(y):

    comfort deluxe, Lou's, 208

    dill dressing, 128

    dill dressing, Carolina crab cakes with, 126–28

    oil dressing, shrimp salad with, 50

    sweet potato puree, 109

lemonade, made-from-scratch, 207

lentil(s):

    cooked, 103

    lima bean circuit hash, 104–5

lima bean(s):

    in butternut squash succotash, 106

    lentil circuit hash, 104–5

limes, in made-from-scratch lemonade, 207

Lou's lemon comfort deluxe, 208

Macaroni:

and cheese, 94

salad, 57

made-from-scratch lemonade, 207

mango:

coconut muffins, 174

in tropical fruit chutney, 79

marinades:

for bourbon-soaked pork chops, 140

brown sugar pineapple jam, 138

buttermilk, *see* buttermilk marinades

chili rub, 75

for corn-crusted porgies, 118–19

for country captain chicken, 162–63

Marv's bay spice, 66

in poached shrimp, 51

in salmon cakes, 116–17

in shrimp cocktail, 36

in vegetable gumbo, 25

Marv's garlic rub, 76

in roast tenderloin of beef with rosemary
and roasted shallot pan gravy, 146–48

Marv's hot sauce, 67

in cold vegetable soup, 31

in Creole sauce, 12–13

Marv spice (savory), 64

in braised red snapper in Creole sauce,
125

in brown rice, 87

in Carolina crab cakes with dill lemon
dressing, 126–28

croutons, 22

in dirty rice, 89

in duck liver spread, 44

in gingersnap-braised chicken, 160

in macaroni and cheese, 94

in macaroni salad, 57

in monkfish and sweet sausage gumbo, 131

in roast pork tenderloin with brown sugar
pineapple jam, 136–38

in salmon cakes, 116–17

in sautéed chicken livers, 43

in stewed chicken, 156–57

Marv's slaw dressing, 55

in cole slaw, 54

Marv's sweet spice, 65

in sweet potato Granny Smith pear stack,
200–201

mascarpone cheese:

in blackened red pepper spread, 77

in Marv's slaw dressing, 55

mash, 97

parsnip, 113

rutabaga carrot, 111

see also puree

mayonnaise, bread-n-butter pickle, 71

meat dishes, 133–52

barbecued short ribs, 134

bourbon-soaked pork chops, 140

braised oxtail, 151–52

chicken-fried steak, 139

grilled filet mignon with brown oyster
gravy, 149–50

pork chops smothered with peppers and
onions, 144–45

roast pork tenderloin with brown sugar
pineapple jam, 136–38

roast tenderloin of beef with rosemary and
roasted shallot pan gravy, 146–48

spare ribs, 135

spicy pulled pork shoulder, 142–43

mint julep, 209

monkfish and sweet sausage gumbo, 131

mud pies, my favorite mini, 186–87

muffins:

    mango coconut, 174

    sweet potato, 175

mussels, in seafood gumbo, 26–27

mustard, three-, barbecue sauce, 14

mustard greens:

    in five-greens rice, 86

    in Frogmore stew, 29–30

my favorite mini mud pies, 186–87

N

Navy bean and okra summer stew, 32–33

O

Okra, 97

    in chicken and sausage gumbo, 28

    in crab and shrimp pilau, 84–85

    in Creole sauce, 12–13

    doubled-dipped fried, 38

    in monkfish and sweet sausage gumbo, 131

    and navy bean summer stew, 32–33

    pickled, 68–69

    in seafood gumbo, 26–27

    in Southern summer ratatouille, 107

    stewed, 102

    in vegetable gumbo, 25

old fashioned, the, 211

onion(s):

    pork chops smothered with peppers and, 144–45

    rings, fried Vidalia, 46–47

orange-honey-glazed grilled Muscovy duck breast, 166–67

oranges, in made-from-scratch lemonade, 207

oxtail, braised, 151–52

oyster hushpuppies, 42

P

Pan-fried catfish, 120–21

pan gravy, 18

pan-seared pompano with Southern summer ratatouille, 124

papaya, in tropical fruit chutney, 79

parsnip:

    mash, 113

    pumpkin, and butternut squash soup, 20–21

peach(es):

    in fresh fruit summer salad, 62

    tea couscous, 96

pear sweet potato Granny Smith stack, 200–201

pecan(s):

    in my favorite mini mud pies, 186–87

    pie, 195

    in praline bread pudding, 188–89

pepper(s):

    pork chops smothered with onions and, 144–45

    spread, blackened red, 77

pickled okra, 68–69

pickled shrimp, 45

pickles, *see* bread-n-butter pickle(s)

pies, pecan, 195

pilau, crab and shrimp, 84–85

pineapple:
  brown sugar jam, 138
  brown sugar jam, roast pork tenderloin
    with, 136–38
  in carrot cake, 196
  and cherry chutney, 78
  in fresh fruit summer salad, 62
  in tropical fruit chutney, 79

poached shrimp, 51

pompano, pan-seared, with Southern summer
    ratatouille, 124

porgies, corn-crusted, 118–19

pork:
  chops, bourbon-soaked, 140
  chops smothered with peppers and onions,
    144–45
  shoulder, spicy pulled, 142–43
  tenderloin with brown sugar pineapple
    jam, roast, 136–38

potato(es), 97
  bread, herbed, 176–77
  in parsnip mash, 113
  salad, 61

potatoes, sweet, *see* sweet potato(es)

poultry, 153–69
  honey-orange-glazed grilled Muscovy
    duck breast, 166–67
  quail with cornbread stuffing, 168–69
  roasted farm-raised guinea hen, 165
  see also chicken

praline bread pudding, 188–89

pumpkin, 97
  parsnip, and butternut squash soup, 20–21

puree:
  celeriac, 112
  lemony sweet potato, 109
  see also mash

Q uail with cornbread stuffing,
  168–69

R ed bell peppers, *see* pepper(s)

red snapper:
  braised, in Creole sauce, 125
  in seafood gumbo, 26–27

rice:
  brown, 87
  coconut, 91
  crab and shrimp pilau, 84–85
  dirty, 89
  five-greens, 86
  golden, 92
  hoppin' John, 83
  spiced, 90
  white, 82
  wild, 88

roast(ed):
  chicken, 158
  corn, 100
  farm-raised guinea hen, 165
  garlic and garlic oil, 73

tropical fruit chutney, 79
trout, buttermilk-dipped, with stewed okra,
123

Veal stock, 7
vegetable(s), 97–113
baby green beans, 101
baked sweet potatoes, 108
butternut squash succotash, 106
celeriac puree, 112
cooked lentils, 103
gumbo, 25
lemony sweet potato puree, 109
lentil lima bean circuit hash, 104–5
parsnip mash, 113
roasted corn, 100
rutabaga carrot mash, 111
sautéed collard greens, 98–99
soup, cold, 31
Southern summer ratatouille, 107
stewed okra, 102
stock, 8
sweet potato fries, 110
see also specific vegetables
vinaigrettes, *see* dressings

Whiskey sour, 212
white balsamic vinaigrette, 59
in asparagus and summer tomato salad,
58
wild rice, 88
wilted greens with herb vinaigrette,
52–53

Yard birds, *see* chicken; poultry
yellow hominy grits, 93
yogurt:
in country captain chicken, 162–63
in gingersnap-braised chicken, 160

Zucchini, in Southern summer ratatouille,
107